LANDMARK MEMORIES

A Vermont Village: 1930s—1950s

❧

LANDMARK MEMORIES

A Vermont Village: 1930s–1950s

～

Joyce Slayton Mitchell

GREEN PLACE BOOKS | *Brattleboro, Vermont*

Printed in the United States

10 9 8 7 6 5 4 3 2 1

GREEN WRITERS PRESS is a Vermont-based publisher whose mission
is to spread a message of hope and renewal through the words and
images we publish. Throughout we will adhere to our commitment to
preserving and protecting the natural resources of the earth. To that
end, a percentage of our proceeds will be donated to environmental,
and social-justice activist groups. Green Writers Press gratefully
acknowledges support from individual donors, friends, and readers to
help support the environment and our publishing initiative. GREEN
PLACE BOOKS curates books that tell literary and compelling stories
with a focus on writing about place.

GREEN
PLACE
BOOKS

Green
writers
press

Giving Voice to Writers & Artists Who Will Make the World a Better Place

Green Writers Press | Brattleboro, Vermont
www.greenwriterspress.com

ISBN: 978-1-9505848-7-1

COVER ARTWORK:
Hazel Hall Rochester, Hardwick, Vermont.

THE PAPER USED IN THIS PUBLICATION IS PRODUCED BY MILLS COMMITTED
TO RESPONSIBLE AND SUSTAINABLE FORESTRY PRACTICES.

For my brother,
John R. Slayton

Special appreciation and thanks to Lorraine Hussey, winner of the 2020 Vermont Historical Society's Award to "recognize the exceptional work done by Lorraine Hussey for the Hardwick Historical Society." Better known in Hardwick as the "go to" person to check everything Hardwick and Hardwick Academy. Lorraine kept the list of H.A. graduates for our alumni banquet held annually until 2017. This author is in a long list of others who came before and currently join me to "ask Lorraine!" No one in the world can match Lorraine's willingness to share her Hardwick memory, as well as her study and scholarship of our *Hardwick Gazette* records from 1859 through today.

Burt Stone, WWII veteran, Hardwick Trust Company, Hardwick Academy and UVM graduate, shared his expertise on fiddleheads, antiques, antique people, and events of Hardwick. My special thanks to Burt's memory and gracious sharing (whether requested or not) for his many notes to me over the years with specific people and dates.

Harold Nunn: Hardwick's radio, TV, and antenna man and a prize deer hunter in Hardwick who knew well and loved Hardwick history. An intense guy, who never spoke unless asked a question. And then—he was a man of great Hardwick stories and detail and has my gratitude for sharing.

Lucinda Rochester Smith, ceramicist, generously gave her permission for photos of her mother's (Hazel Hall Rochester) paintings to be included in *Landmark Memories*. Lucinda's time given in formatting and discussing the paintings included in this book are beyond measure. Thank you, Lucinda.

CONTENTS

∾

LANDMARK MEMORIES

A Vermont Village: 1930s—1950s

❧

MEET HARDWICK:

Population: 1200

◦∕

A VILLAGE with everything anyone ever needed: a school, several churches, a library, a whole Main Street of stores, a livery stable, a Post Office, a town band, a beautiful gym for everyone to play basketball, a bowling alley, two drug stores, two 5 and 10 cent stores, a hardware store, and a meat market where fresh fish came in every Friday. And oh—a lot of places to eat. Did I mention a pool hall?

Hardwick was a Northeast Kingdom village in those days where kids could walk, run, slide, scooter, or bike anywhere as long as they were home at their dinner table at 12 noon and supper table at 5:30. If your father didn't know where you were, some other grown-up would know. As a child in Hardwick, if I were somewhere I shouldn't be, playing with kids who lived on another street at 5:30 p.m. when all of us should be home at our own supper tables, all the grown-up had to say was, "Does your father know where you are?" The game was forgotten for the fastest run home. If I wanted to play in the town band and didn't have an instrument to play or know how to blow a trumpet, Mrs. Hooper, the town librarian, found a trumpet in her attic and gave it to me to use until I graduated, 6 years later. Bill Robb, from our post office, taught all of us kids who wanted to play the brasses, how to play our instruments and march in the Town Band on Memorial Day and the 4th of July. Hardwick was too small to have a separate school band. Oh yes, Will Johnson, the Postmaster, taught the rest of the kids how to play the reeds. No one had to teach the drums.

If a kid didn't find his mother home after school, he could call Elva Archer, our telephone operator, and ask her where his mother was. It was where, after supper in the summertime, there were kids playing "Kick the Can" in the middle of West Church Street, or a pick-up game of baseball with Jack Hall, the manager of the granite sheds, umpiring while several of our parents sat visiting on their front porch and watching us.

Grown-ups and kids were all mixed up in school events—the town band, sports, parades, auctions, and daily life. If the 3rd grade teacher told you in school how great FDR was, your father might send you right back to school after dinner to tell her that FDR sold our country down the river. Daily life for a Hardwick child was pretty much the same rules at home, in school and church, and in between.

In those years, PTA meetings, Town Meetings, churches, Masons, Eastern Star ladies, as well as the Knights of Columbus and Kiwanis Club had full memberships. Our parents and all grown-ups governed Hardwick's town, school, churches, and service clubs—they showed up for town meeting the first Tuesday in March to vote on our school and road budgets. Those years were Vermont's Republican days (and they still are in the Northeast Kingdom). Our renowned U.S. Republican Senator George D. Aiken served Vermont well. From 1942 to 1975. Republicans in the 30s, 40s, and 50s were economically conservative and socially liberal.

Landmark Memories are stories of community living, reminding us of how our Vermont villages linked people so solidly together. A place where grown-ups volunteered to start a band, take children hunting, fishing, skiing—where grown-ups, whether they had children or not, showed up at Hardwick Academy's basketball games and Junior Proms, and taught us things, such as how to play musical instruments for the band, how to march like a soldier during WWII, how to build a fire in the snow. Things like that.

More than historical pieces of a village, *Landmark Memories* are examples to the world of how people of all ages lived together in our towns and cities. Stories from the 1930s, when the author was born and at three years old, was so happy to be in a 1936 WPA pre-school program run by Clara Travers. Having a snack of tomato juice with a graham cracker is memorable—in the Methodist Church with those beautiful stained-glass windows. It was right across the street from our Town Offices in our beautiful granite Memorial Building—and kitty-corner from our red-stone Lambert Packard-designed Jeudevine Library.

In the early 1940s, when I was about ten years old, I asked my father why we had to live in such a small little town in the middle of nowhere. Nowhere? We live two hours from Montreal where the best French pastries are. We live four hours from Boston where there's a Chinatown to get crab dumplings and BBQ spareribs. We live eight hours from New York City, where we can get hot pastrami on rye and real dill pickles—the greatest city in the world. Why, little girl, you live in the center of the world!

Dear readers: Meet Hardwick, Vermont . . . in the "Center of the world!"

I Remember

∽

DOWNSTREET

DOWNSTREET. Hardwick's home base. Hardwick's center is at the "Dummy," the 3-way intersection in the middle of the road. Where Rt. # 15—from Burlington in the West to Maine in the East—goes through Hardwick, and North Main Street meets Main Street and leaves town as South Main toward our capital, Montpelier. This memorable Dummy, a cement circle, is about two feet high, topped with a green iron corrugated column at least 6 feet high and crowned with a global-shaped lamp. Our school patrol used to stand there to protect us on our way to and from school. The Dummy marks the triangle where Cox's Drugstore (and Soda Fountain) stands on one point, our Post Office across the street and the Hardwick Inn completes the triangle.

It wasn't until 1963, that we had or knew names for all our streets. That's when America was divided up into zip codes. We didn't use street names, except for our own street. I never heard anybody say, "I'm going up or down to Main Street." If we lived north of the Lamoille, we walked over to the library and then downstreet. My best friends Kay and Clare lived down on Cottage Street, on the South side of the Lamoille River. They said, "we'll meet you Upstreet." If kids lived on other streets, I don't know what they said.

"Downstreet" and "Upstreet" means restaurants, our movie theatre, and Eva Bemis's 5 and 10 cent store, Charlie Morse's pool hall, and Mr. Battles's and Lila Racette's dress shops. Our mothers sometimes went to the dress shops, and not often our fathers bought gifts for our mothers there—to be returned later. There were no children's shops simply because our mothers made our clothes, or we had hand -me-downs from older siblings, cousins, or neighbors.

Next was Eaton's Meat Market, where fresh fish came in every Friday for the Catholics. My father said that "Catholics don't like fish because they have to eat it, and so the Protestants plan on fresh fish every Friday." Right in the middle of "Downstreet," across from the pool hall and Bruno's restaurant, is our renowned "Swinging Bridge," crossing the Lamoille

River. It was built in 1916 for the workers at Daniel's manufacturing of wood-burning furnaces. It smelled like tar around that building. Bopsy Daniel's father must have used tar to hold the furnaces together. We sometimes grabbed a piece of that black, shiny, rubbery tar off the ground and chewed it. It stuck to our teeth like spruce gum.

As kids walked, skipped, and ran over the swinging bridge, we could see the water rushing below. We could feel the swing of the cables holding us up. Big kids liked to pump their knees making the bridge go up and down, scaring little kids as we ran across.

The Hardwick Gazette building is next to the bridge and the back of it looked like it hung out over the river. The Swinging Bridge was most important for kids on West Church Street because it was the short-cut to Hardwick Academy, which was at the top of Main Street on the left going out of town. Last on Main were the Catholic and United Churches—white steeples facing off against each other on opposite sides of Main Street on Congo Hill.

If, at the Dummy, we went left instead of up Main, there was Art Bacon's barber shop—it used to be Burt Cobb's barber shop—and then Freddy Shattuck's paper store, followed by a bowling alley and a hardware store where I could buy a dime's worth of 10-penny nails.

When we hurried off to school on those cold, early mornings, kids on West Church Street had two choices . . . to go through the hole in Ruby Spier's fence over to Highland Avenue by Blaine and Maud Grow's house, scoot over past the undertaker, Mr. Peck, and finally, cut a fast track, down the hill by Daniel's furnace manufacturing, run across the Swinging Bridge, and we'd be half way up Main Street, three running minutes to our school's front door.

Or, after dinner, most days we walked back along with the grown-ups who lived on West Church St. and were headed back to work. Those days we'd walk up to the library, and then downstreet to Main St. Before the Dummy, Mr. Ladd and Dr. Beaupré would take a left on Mill Street past Mrs. Parker's piano and furniture store in the same building as the Post Office. Dr. Beaupre's dentist office was upstairs in the bank building, one of the few brick buildings in Hardwick. I remember smelling the "laughing gas" on the steep stairs warning us kids of the dentist office. Mr. Spaulding's studio, the photographer, was on the third and top floor.

Downstreet was Hardwick's entertainment in the days when life was centered around home, school, church, and sports. The movies were downstreet. The pool halls, bowling alley, restaurants, and the excitement of comings and goings in all those stores and activities were downstreet. There were no sports on Saturday night. Downstreet was the place to be— mixing us all up from every street and neighboring villages. The young mesmerized by the Queen of the Mountain being driven downstreet by horse and wagon or sleigh, depending on the season. And by old Sarah Allen in her long black skirt, long-sleeved black blouse and brimmed, black hat shouting out at us in front of Cox's Drug Store for Hardwick souls to Repent! And be Saved! Oh yes! There was only one place to be on Saturday nights in Hardwick. Downstreet.

I Remember

❧

OUR ICEMAN:
HARLAND E. ROWELL

Bub

HE CAME to Hardwick from Mackville, Mackville Pond. He married Jennie Dodge who came to Hardwick from Johnson to teach school. Bub had everything a man could want . . . a family with a son and daughter, a home on Church Street, a deer camp on Woodbury Mountain (beside the Queen of the Mountain), and a fishing camp on Caspian Lake.

It was from Bub Rowell that I learned what an "easy-going" person is. He smiled more than he talked. He sauntered into all of our homes in the mid-30s and early '40s, leather ice carrier over his shoulder filled with the chunk of ice that would fit just right into the top of our ice box. Remember that pan of water underneath that someone had to empty each day? Bub had a red Ford pick-up with scales on the back and a heavy, grey canvas covering the ice. He measured and chipped, whistling while he worked. The ice came off Mackville pond, where his dad had cut ice before him, cut in the proper-sized squares, then stored in their Mackville barn, covered with straw so it wouldn't melt in the summer.

Living right across the street from Bub Rowell, I often sat on the high stool near their breakfast nook, as they called it. It was a bench instead of chairs on one side; no one else had one of those on Church Street, but the Robbs had one just like it on Cottage Street. I don't know why they called it their breakfast nook as they ate every single meal there except for Thanksgiving and Christmas dinner when Bub's brother Carroll and his mother drove in from Mackville. And Jennie's brother, Dick Dodge, and his family from Johnson.

I remember whenever my parents or the Ladds or Halls had a party, they always counted on Bub to take care of the heavy drinkers. A big guy, he would put his arm over their shoulders and quietly say, "Now Harry, let's take a little walk home." No one ever got fighting words out of Bub Rowell. He was gentle. He could persuade anyone to let him walk or drive him home.

Bub is the guy who had a chocolate milkshake every single day in Cox's Drug Store on the corner stool by the window.

Bub is the guy who always had a deer camp story to tell about his best friend, Wheeler. He loved his fishing at Caspian and trolled for lakers at dawn and dusk all summer long.

Bub could sing. While Jennie sat at their upright piano jumping around and playing all the old favorites as fast as she could, Bub just stood still, leaned down, sang away nice and easy. I remember best, "I Want to Go Home."

After the Hardwick people bought refrigerators in the '40s at the end of the war, Bub became the chief of police. He was always a volunteer fireman. At the same time, Bub bought Hardwick's Idle Hour Theatre. He ran it with the same rules for us kids as Mr. Carr had run the movie theatre. That means that we children had to sit in the first six rows and had to be quiet. We were policed with a flashlight. And junior high kids were never allowed to go into the balcony. Gene Autry and Roy Rogers were the Western cowboys on Friday and Saturday nights, and the best movies that our parents saw were with Spencer Tracy, Gregory Peck, and Betty Davis on Sunday nights. It was impossible to make that Sunday night movie and attend Young People's or

CYO. Finally, the churches gave in and had our youth groups meet earlier so we could run down and make the 7 o'clock show.

Bub had just the personal skills and temperament necessary to be the perfect Town Manager. I remember often hearing his end of the telephone conversation in their kitchen. During breakfast or after supper when an irate Hardwickian called to yell at him about their road not being plowed or the impossible road during mud season, his smooth voice would say, "Now Floyd, we are going to get up there the first thing in the morning." He would listen and listen, say half a sentence in his calm, reassuring voice, hang up, turn to Jennie, shaking his head, and say, "That was Floyd again. Let's see, that's his fourth call this week . . ."

I remember walking to school in the morning and hearing that "Bub took Thelma Baker over to Waterbury last night." I pictured him going into her house in the middle of the night, persuading Thelma that the best thing she could do for herself was to get in the car with him for a ride over to Waterbury, our State Insane Asylum.

I remember when the town manager was in charge of the poor farm. Wasn't that on Hardwick Lake by the pest house and slaughterhouse? After the poor farm went out of fashion, surplus food for the poor was stored in Bub's barn right outside his wood-working shop. That's where people came and asked for food as they needed it.

The last time I saw Bub Rowell, he was sitting at camp in his favorite chair, the sun shining down on him from across the lake and his familiar smile shining up at me as I stood there talking away about fishing and went on and on about everyone we both knew.

I remember Bub most of all as a content man who served his family and Hardwick, Vermont. It was from Bub Rowell that I learned what public service means. And kindness, too.

I Remember

❧

W. S. Bemis
HARDWICK'S
5 & 10 CENT STORE

A DIME gripped safely in my 6-year old hand, dressed in my warmest snowsuit and overshoes, I started across West Church Street toward the library, down the hill over the green iron bridge, heading toward W.S. Bemis 5 and 10 cent store on February 21 to buy my mother's February 22nd birthday present. The first gift I ever bought. I knew exactly what I was going to buy. I had spent hours prowling the aisles, looking up at those counters edged and divided by glass panels, collecting my options for gifts I knew my mother would love. There it was. I stood on tiptoe, reaching up and over the glass edge and chose the cobalt blue bottle of "Evening in Paris."

A long, slender bottle about three inches tall with a blue string and tassel around its throat decorated this most elegant gift in all of Hardwick.

In second grade, my classmates and I bought our valentines at Hardwick's 5 and 10. We bought a few individual ones, but most of us bought a "do it yourself" book with 25 valentines and envelopes that we cut and pasted because we needed a lot of them. Our teacher, Mrs. McKenna, made a Valentine's Day Post Office in her classroom that she constructed every single year for her second graders. Every kid got mail on Valentine's Day.

Even though I had thought that the store had been there forever, W. S. Bemis didn't open until 1925 in a brand-new building when Hardwick's Main Street was rebuilt after the big fire of July 2, 1923. Ed Appolt and C.P. Davis built the store. At the same time, Raleigh Battles and Homer Caukins went into their new stores: Battles into dresses and Caukins into dry goods You can go in now and look up at the original 1925 off-white, patterned tin ceilings.

To learn the ropes, Eva and Waldo went to New York City for their first buying trip with the Parkers from Springfield (Vermont) who were already in the 5 and 10 cent store business. The Bemis's knew them because Mrs. Parker was Florence Nelson, a Hardwick woman who married and moved to Springfield. The two couples continued to work together, going back and forth and helping each other out with special sales, pricing, and buying. On opening day in 1925, 50 to 60 people showed up at the new 5 and 10 cent store.

In the 1940s, every woman in Hardwick bought a new Easter hat. Immediately to the right as you walked in the door, you could see a mirror in the middle of the counter surrounded by the Easter collection of straws and ribbons, small hats with veils, flowers in front, back, and on top of this exquisite collection hanging on pegs surrounding the mirror. Easter hats for little girls cost $3.98, and a pair of gloves sold for a dollar. The cash register area was alive with chocolate Easter bunnies, and jellybeans by the bulk. I still have my mother's tiny, yellow, fluffy-cotton, Easter chicks made in Japan, and sold before the war on that counter next to the cash register.

Soon after they got started, Waldo decided he didn't like store work, so he left it to Eva and went off to be a carpenter with Joe Lavertu. He then expanded his block and eventually his renters numbered 25 apartments, 4 stores, a successful pool hall in the basement of one building, plus the telephone company on the second floor. He loved the challenge of figuring out how to heat all four buildings with one central furnace, and the maintenance of his Main

Street acquisitions. The only thing Waldo never gave up at the store was decorating the windows. Eva could always count on him to come up with something original. One year he pasted real dollar bills all over the windows for "Dollar Day." That made a big splash in Hardwick. Special merchandise was purchased for Dollar Days, Eva remembers buying metal pails for the first specials.

Memorial Day was big business at Bemis's 5 and 10. The store's biggest sellers in the whole year were the boxes of flowers and flags for the graves. There were two prices on those Memorial Day flowers, $1.49 and $1.98. Eva said they could count on selling 600 boxes. That's a lot of flowers for a village of 1200 people!

But of course, W. S. Bemis wasn't just for Hardwick folks. The Greensboro summer people made a big difference in summer sales. And many customers came from Greensboro, East Hardwick, Wolcott, Woodbury, Craftsbury, Walden, Stannard, and Calais to the only 5 and 10 cent store around. Eva says that oftentimes, out-of-towners would come in the early afternoon, hang up their coats down in back by the big mirror, and stay the whole afternoon, looking things over. After all, there were 3 floors to shop! Toys upstairs, hardware and wallpaper downstairs, and the main floor of hats, dresses, raincoats, and shoes besides cosmetics, school supplies, and candy. And before the war, you could even find imported souvenir china cups and saucers, salt and peppers from Germany with "Hardwick" written on them.

The bookkeeping perch, down in back, up the stairs, is where I remember seeing Eva, bent over her books. She often came down those wooden, ladder-like stairs and wandered around the aisles. Her right-hand clerk, Nancy Fisher, started working on the first day the store opened and worked 51 weeks a year, getting one week off for vacation. Later, Betty Riach was the number one clerk, whom I remember from the 1940s. Betty waited on customers and dusted all those glass dividers while Eva did the books. She changed things around, so the color crayons and candy or hosiery, or playing cards were never in the same place for very long.

Besides the retail trade, Mayme Weeks—who taught school in Wolcott and Woodbury before she put in fifty years at our Jackson Bridge School—and other teachers bought their students' Christmas presents at Eva's store. Once Hardwick's 5 and 10 cent store opened, Jennie Goodenough ordered all of her scotch tape, paper clips, and pencils from them. Jennie started teaching in the South Walden School in 1915 and taught all 8 grades for 60 years.

Memorial Day over, Mother's Day whirled in, bringing sales of more cotton-printed housedresses in one holiday than were sold for the rest of the year. Eva sold hundreds of cotton dresses at $2.98. Even George Fisher bought one of those housedresses for his common-law wife, Hazel, Queen of the Mountain, on Mother's Day. A lot of candy was sold, too, for Mother's Day. There were chocolate-covered peach blossoms by the bulk, and boxes of chocolates for every holiday of the season.

Besides Christmas, kids loved Decoration Day best. The 4th of July brought fireworks to the store in the days when they were legal. I remember a card-table set out on the sidewalk of the 5 and 10. It was loaded down with colorful packages of firecrackers from China packaged in shiny, thin green or red or purple papers. There were boxes of caps, cap guns, roman candles, and sparklers, of course. I can still smell the distinctive smell of the smoke from those caps exploding on the hot metal of the silver cap guns that all of us kids had.

Everyone in Hardwick knew summer was over by the Labor Day softball game and picnic down in West End. But we had already seen the 5 and 10 cent store windows filled with school things. The rubberized book bag had that "ready for school" smell, with a pencil pouch on the side. I remember looking over the glass edge and selecting a brand new 3-ring notebook, pencils, a pencil box, and a separate package of paper for my new notebook.

Even though most of us made our own costumes to go to the Halloween party in the gym for the whole town, we did buy Halloween corn kernels-candy and masks. The Bemis's could count on October sales being good because the Kiwanis Club bought their Halloween door prizes and party prizes from them every year.

The Bemis's didn't take a vacation for the first 25 years of business. After the first 25 years, Eva and Waldo took a week off in the spring and another one in October before the Christmas season. Betty Riach held down the store. Only once did they go away for more than a week. Thirty-one years after they opened the store, they took a 3-week trip out West in 1961. Waldo never once gave it a thought; Eva never once had a day without thinking of her store. She loved the customers and being in the public. She loved the buying trips to New York City and going to all the latest Broadway musicals, staying at the New Yorker, going to Louchows and Mama Leone's for dinner. Eva never got sick of the store.

Eva says that practically every girl in high school worked for her at one time or another. She hired 3 each summer and at Christmas time there were 8 clerks. My Aunt Eunice worked for Eva one Christmas holiday when she was at UVM.

The biggest excitement of all at the store, though, was the radio given away on Christmas Eve. A beautiful floor model Philco Radio. Fifty to sixty customers gathered around in the store for the big event and at exactly 11:00 p.m. just before Midnight Mass, someone from the crowd stepped forward to draw the winning number, and the lucky family won the Philco! It was the best marketing strategy in town.

Hardwick's 5 and 10 Cent Store. Growing up in Hardwick we knew that the first sign of a season or holiday was reflected through the Bemis's windows. In 1945, the year the Hardwick Village Restaurant was built right across the street, an out-of-town woman came out of the restaurant, saw the Christmas windows, and went straight over to report that she had never seen a more beautiful Christmas window . . . not even in Burlington.

I Remember

❧

MRS. COBB: ENGLISH, FRENCH AND LATIN TEACHER

"Children, children, it's time for class to begin!" said Mrs. Cobb, without ever thinking of raising her voice as she clapped her tiny hands together to get our attention. Every single student, even the rowdiest boys who hated school, paid attention for learning English from five-foot (maybe) tall Mrs. Cobb, our only 9th and 10th grade English teacher. That was in the late 40s, when she stood up in front of us reading *The Ancient Mariner* and *Evangeline*. When Mrs. Cobb read to us, no one would dare whisper or throw a paper or pass a note or kick a classmate under the desk. We paid attention whether we liked the story or not. She commanded our respect at all times and in turn, she respected us. Well, probably it was the other way around. Even as other teachers would complain about this one or that in our class, she would say, "Why I can't understand it, Ernest or Mabel, or Ira acts alright in my class." She didn't get sick of us even when she had some of us for six years: two years of English, two of Latin, and two of French. She encouraged us all, but especially the French-Canadian boys from the farms. They had just started to come down to the village for high school. Their sisters had to stay home and take care of the younger children and help their mother with 8 to 12 children in a family on the farm.

Mrs. Cobb encouraged us all, even with her special affinity for those French students. She just smiled all over when "Peasoup" Renaud danced into the room, Denis LeBlanc charmed her, and Robert Lecours was just plain her favorite—he always strode seriously into the classroom, all business, just like Mrs. Cobb.

But the classroom isn't the first thing I remember about Mrs. Cobb. The very first image I have of her, about 1937, was when she was curling her daughter Sarah's hair. Sarah was my first friend, my neighbor. When I ran over to get Sarah to come out and play, I had to sit there and wait until Mrs. Cobb meticulously brushed her hair into Shirley Temple ringlets. I had pigtails and they were a lot faster for my mother to braid each morning.

The Cobbs were well known in Hardwick because a "Carl Cobb house" meant a well-built house with the best of lumber and design, as were the Bridgman houses. I know the Bridgman houses because my grandmother lived up the hill across from the circus field in a Bridgman house, known for its interior of curly maple woodwork—even the stairs. We lived in a Cobb house. These houses were turn of the century and Hardwick's finest homes.

There were three "Cobb" houses on West Church Street in the early 1900s. Carl Cobb was Sarah's great uncle. His brother-in-law, Mr. Brown, lived on West Church Street in a Cobb house. The president of the bank, Mr. Ladd, and his family bought the Brown house in the 1940s. The Holcombe's, Hardwick's other undertaker, lived in another, and Burt and Bertha Cobb lived in the third Cobb house on West Church. My Dad bought the Holcomb house when my younger brother, John, was born in 1943 and we moved down four houses, now on the other side of Sarah's house. I was still only one house away—and now in a Cobb house.

When the Cobbs lived on Church Street, Mrs. Cobb didn't teach school. I don't remember when they moved to "the other side of the tracks," as Sarah's younger brother Roscoe, used to say to the annoyance of his family and their friends. Roscoe was in my class, their third child Carl, was born much later—and that's probably when they bought a house further away for their three children.

By the time her children were all in school and Mrs. Cobb went back to teaching, I was in Junior High School. I do know that she was the talk of the town because Mrs. Cobb went to the school board (Jack Hall) to say it wasn't right that an experienced teacher earned less than $3,000 a year just because she already lived in Hardwick. The new young University of Vermont graduates who didn't know a thing about teaching came in and started over $3,000. What I admired most about Mrs. Cobb was that she was the fairest teacher I ever had. Besides that, probably because of it, Mrs. Cobb was a woman who stood up for her rights, even when she didn't have a chance of winning them.

I Remember

∿

THE UNITED CHURCH
OF HARDWICK

Was anything more exciting to a 5-year old than opening new patent-leather Mary-Jane shoes, with a surprise bag of marbles in the shoebox, early on Easter morning for the Sunrise Service in the United Church of Hardwick? Getting to Church by 6:00 a.m., smelling the wafting scents of pancakes and sausages being cooked during the service, imaging the taste of this season's new maple syrup, hearing the choir's sunrise Hosannas and Hallelujahs, feeling that Easter and spring are here and that the Church and all of Hardwick is once again renewed. Winter must be over. Or almost over. No matter the weather, the hope and promise of spring never let us down on Easter morning.

And when grown up enough to be past the marble-playing age, Easter Sunday turned into a fashion parade. Protestant met Catholic friends right after the 11 a.m. services of Mass directly across the street, to walk all around our village taking photos of each other with our Brownie box cameras in our homemade or hand-me-down three-quarter length spring coats and new Easter hats, bought at Bemis's 5 and 10 cent store. My Junior High School photo album is filled with Easter photos of my best friends, Kay O'Malley and Clare Robb, in their Easter outfits.

The Easter Play was a major dramatic event for the adults of the United Church. Mrs. George Jenkins, director of the play, Carroll Rowell, Sally Slayton, and Agnes and Irwin Hoxie were among the stars in the play. It was a full production with elaborate sets and fine costumes which played to a full house.

John Chester Smith was the first minister I remember. He came to the United Church in 1938, although my mother had photos of Bob White, the former minister, lifting me on the palm of his hand, as a toddler. The Slaytons lived next door to the parsonage. Rev. White was the first minister called when the United Church of Hardwick came into being by uniting Hardwick's Baptists,

Congregationalists, and Methodists. Even though the original Congregational Church was "United" in 1931, and Mr. Smith was a Baptist, still, we were told when we went out of Vermont to just say we were Congregationalists.

Our church was best known to every kid in Hardwick for the fastest sliding hill in town. Congo Hill was closed off from cars and sanding, and children could be found there right after school and on Saturday mornings with their flexible fliers, homemade sleds, and several lucky kids had a traverse. One kid made a single ski with a seat "scooter." Toboggans were used only on our hilly fields. The daredevils started their run across Main Street, right in the middle of the road, sled in hand, rope carefully tucked between the slats so it wouldn't drag and slow the slide. Running as fast as they could they slammed the sled to the snow-covered road just at the crest, leaped on their sled as a diver hits the water in a swim meet. They could get all the way past Elm Street with that jump-start from the middle of the road.

The Congregational Church was originally built on South Main in 1896 (although the Congregationalists started meetings in the old Fire House on Main Street, in 1893). The Baptist Church, also on South Main, was built in 1893, joined us along with the most beautiful of all, the Bethany Methodist Episcopal Church up on Church Street next to the Sullivan house. The Methodists organized in Hardwick as early as 1803 and built their magnificent building in 1847. The clock face on all four sides of its tower was given to the town by Mrs. A.F. Jeudevine in 1889, and the dramatic, columned portico was a gift from Mrs. L.D. Hathaway. After 1935 it was used for town rather than religious purposes, and many of us will remember the summer recreation and preschool programs in the old Methodist Church. If I could bring back to Hardwick any building—thinking of all that we have lost by fire or demolition: Four churches, Hardwick Academy, and the Idle Hour Theatre, Cox's Drug Store, and the Eagle Hotel—I would bring back the Methodist Church with the clock face that could be seen and heard from almost everywhere in Hardwick.

I don't know why the Congregational Church was chosen as the place for the United Church to be . . . maybe because it had the biggest pipe organ in town? We had three choirs in Mr. Smith's days. Marion Shattuck was the first Junior Choir Director in 1939. We were dressed in white robes with red ties, made by our Hardwick librarian, Mrs. Hooper. Mrs. Florence Lane was the organist, as well as Hardwick's piano lessons teacher—in her home—50 cents a lesson. She also directed the choir and played the organ every Sunday through the 1930s, '40s, and '50s. I remember when Mrs. Lane and Fran Holcomb played organ and piano duets for special occasions. Mrs. Holcomb remembers it well, especially rehearsals, in the days when the building was heated only on Sunday, and it was so cold at rehearsal during the week that she and Mrs. Lane practiced with their gloves on.

The music that I most clearly remember was centered around Mrs. Hooper. She often sang soprano solos, as well as many duets with alto Joanna Lyford; and quintets with Leota Hoyt, Mrs. Gertrude Battles, and Mrs. Florence Lane. Before I was old enough to join the Junior Choir, I remember falling asleep during the sermon on my mother's arm, gazing up at the patterned tin ceiling, feeling the warmth of the faded red velvet curtain in front of the choir loft, following the curve of the smooth, light-colored wood pews.

I have a treasured copy of Louisa May Alcott's *Little Women*, inscribed in Mr. Smith's hand for "excellent attendance" in 1941. Mrs. Esther Morse (the first "Saint" I had ever heard of) was the Superintendent of Sunday School, and Sarah Peck (Sal Densmore) one of the Sunday School teachers. In those days, even though he was our closest neighbor, Mr. Smith paid a formal, annual visit to our family. I can well remember standing in our living room in a circle as he held our family in prayer. I could never figure out how he got my dad to stand in that circle! Mr. Smith was a calm, low-keyed, persuasive, handsome man, bringing many improvements to our village church that he believed were needed. After visiting the sick, he would often go home and say to Mrs. Smith, "That family needs a nurse more than they need a minister!" And being a man of the scripture, ". . . be ye doers of the word, and not hearers only" (James 1:22), he wrote a grant proposal to the Terrill Foundation, in Burlington. Hardwick soon had our first community nurse. Mrs. Marian Bandon arrived in the early 1940s with her two sons, Paul and David. She lived in the Nelson house, the last house on West Church Street, across from the Morse and Libby house (John Hall's present house). Her brother, the Rev. Roderick Hurlbert, followed her to Hardwick to become the third minister of the United Church from 1944 through 1949. Following Mrs. Brandon was Dorothy Kibbee, also on the Church staff. After that time, the Town of Hardwick took over the financial responsibility of Hardwick's community nurse, and the first one was Sal Densmore's sister, Ava Peck (the undertaker's daughter, and doctor's sister-in-law. I won't mention what my dad thought of going to a doctor whose father-in-law was the undertaker).

The Board of Directors of the United Church in the early 1940s included Judge Morse, Will and Della Marshall, Raleigh Battles, Oscar Shepard, Gerald Ladd, and Guy Larrabee.

Listening to a hymn chime at exactly 6:00 p.m. throughout Hardwick while playing tennis on the Hazen Union courts in the 1990s reminds me of Mr. Smith's talent for encouraging gifts to the church—for development. The chimes were a gift to the United Church from Mrs. Della Marshall just before World War II. An endowment for the Marshall Fund college scholarship to the United Church followed the chimes. Margaret Larrabee was the first one I remember who received it. She did the church and Hardwick Academy proud, graduating with a perfect 4.0 average from UVM!

As a youngster in the church, the biggest event of the year, after Easter and Christmas, was the Mother and Daughter banquet. Sybil (Messier) and Janet (Slayton) Houston both remember it best because the "men did all the work!" They cooked and waited on tables. That was a sight to see and only happened once a year. When my mother died, I found amongst her few souvenirs a program of the Mother and Daughter banquet from 1942 when we were both on the program: She presented one of her dramatic monologues for which she was known, and I read one of her favorite poems by Edgar A. Guest. Of course, there was a Father and Son banquet, too, but the women doing all the cooking and serving wasn't anything new.

In the 1940s, every Hardwick Academy student belonged to the Catholic or Protestant church, and the minister and priest came to school one afternoon a week for religious education. A few years later, we were let out of school early to cross the street to get our religious education at church. A vacation Bible School was held for a month in the summer, we had bible study in the morning, and parents drove us to Lake Eligo in the afternoons. I remember the only summer I ever rode in a beach wagon (a "demonstrator" from my father's Ford garage) with real leather seats and beech wood on the outside. My mother drove our class to Lake Eligo for swimming and a picnic lunch. Cold from swimming, we rushed for the wagon, smelling and feeling the warmth of the sun on those hot leather seats.

I remember the first (and last) child's funeral I ever attended at the United Church. Carla Clark had been killed in a sliding accident. Many of Hardwick's 9-, 10-, and 11-year-olds were there. I remember that none of us ever talked about the funeral—about death—or heaven or what happens when you die.

The church was a major institution for teenage

social life in Vermont. We often went to or invited the "Young People" of Craftsbury and Greensboro to our Sunday evenings, and went to Stowe for programs with their teens. Young Peoples' met on Sunday evening (many of us remember the controversy at home of Sunday night movies vs. Young Peoples'). The movies won out, as the church finally set our meeting early enough so that we could all attend, and then "run to beat the band" just in time to catch the 7 o'clock movie.

It was through the church that teenagers got around. We met other students all over the state at summer camps, conferences, and on special trips. In summer, a few of us went to Camp Teela Wooket, in Roxbury for a week. I even remember meeting a cousin for the first time—the cutest boy with the best smile in the whole camp. When I got home and at the supper table, I told my folks his name, my father asked, "Arnold Tebbetts from Cabot? Why, your great grandmother is his grandfather's sister—his father and my father are own cousins. He's your second cousin, once removed!" Oh no . . .

I remember meeting Doris Kingsley at a retreat at the Atkinson House in Newbury. She was a lay preacher, whose ministry was teenage leadership for rural Vermont communities. Marjorie Davis, Keith Ladd, and I often went off for weekends with her,

joining others from Southern Vermont to give ser-
mons in churches without a pastor. A New England
Camp at Lake Winnipesaukee took us to a confer-
ence with young people from all over the country
where I met my first Black friend. And my first trip
to the United Nations in New York City where I
heard Eleanor Roosevelt speak—all through the
sponsorship of the United Church of Hardwick.

The Rev. Granville Greenwald was the last minister of the 1940s, who took the United Church into
the 1950s. He must have felt a real Young Peoples'
mission, because he took us for ski trips to Stowe
(even though he had never been on skis), on camping
and hiking trips, and we drove to conferences way
down to Manchester and all over the state in his station wagon filled with teenagers.

I remember outsiders coming to the United
Church. Missionaries from Africa showed their
slides and told us of their exciting life in exotic places.
The Reverend Eugene Carter, Associate Pastor of
New York City's Riverside Church, who summered
in Greensboro, often spoke at our Young People's
evenings. And when the Riverside Church Choir
came from New York City to sing for the United
Church, the best voice and most beautiful of them
all—Bronwyn Potter—never went back! She simply
married a Vermont farmer and stayed here forever.

I remember Hardwick's United Church. It's the church I grew up in, where I was sent to Sunday School, where my father would ask me what I had learned and then argue every point with me, sending me back the following Sunday with his arguments for which I would predictably be sent home for my irreverence. This is the very same church where I was baptized, became an active teenage member, where I was married, and my parents buried.

Even though that old Congo Hill building was destroyed by fire, and a new one replaced it in 1975, still, I never get through a Sunday Service now without hearing Jennie Rowell's alto voice leaning toward me to give me my note in the choir, seeing Mrs. Lane at the organ, peeking at Mr. Davis and Mr. Cobb standing in front for the offering prayer, smelling the Holcomb's Easter lilies filling the air, and feeling the presence of my parents and their friends, as they raised their voices in Hardwick's United Church on Easter Sunday morning.

I Remember

❧

MY AUNT MURIEL

"Who the hell wants their hair curled now?" was her typical response to the ringing phone. "But that's not what I want to talk about," was her response to any statement that didn't hit dead center of what she had in mind. "I want to talk about what Muriel wants to talk about," quickly followed if you were on the wrong track.

Glamorous, opinionated, a handsome woman, brave, opinionated, entrepreneur, doing things her way, difficult, opinionated, impossible, outrageous, and opinionated are words that come to mind as I remember my Aunt Muriel.

I first remember her driving an Oldsmobile into my grandparents' yard in Hardwick. Even at ten years old, I knew well that no Slayton would dream of driving, much less owning, anything other than a Ford. The family business is Ford. Ford was brought to Hardwick in the late 1920s by my grandfather, Aunt Muriel's and my dad's father. It was then lost to the bank in the depression, and bought back by my father in 1931, the year he was married. Oh yes, my Aunt Muriel loved driving that beautiful, big, black Oldsmobile to Hardwick into a Slayton yard. She was in a fur coat, sunglasses (I had never seen sunglasses on anyone before except in the movies). At her side was her red and white, short-haired dog, Jacko-de-hound. My brother Jay and I watched in awe, as Betty Davis came to mind.

Fiercely independent. She rented an apartment and had her own beauty shop at nineteen years old in St. Johnsbury, with a kitchen, bedroom, and a few steps leading up to the bathroom in back of the shop. She was the only person I knew who lived in an apartment in a city (population, 6,000) building. She was married to a man as handsome and charming as she was independent.

I remember the family telling that Aunt Muriel quit UVM and Johnson Normal School to go into business. Besides her St. J. shop, she opened a part-time beauty shop in Bethlehem, New Hampshire to cash in on the summer tourist business. In our long, cold winters, Aunt Muriel piled her curling equipment into her car to go to women's homes to do their perms.

I can remember her summer cottage right on the shore front of Partridge Lake (we pronounced it Patridge Lake) in New Hampshire, the first family member to have a summer place. It was at the cottage that I first heard of a "spaghetti feed," and the first time I ever tasted spicy hot. I stayed overnight many times in that cottage, rowed the boat, fished for perch, and remembered her neighbors, the Downings, whom she so admired. I also remember a handsome photographer, her man of Partridge Lake. When driving to Littleton now, there is a sign to Partridge Lake, reminding me of my childhood image of my successful aunt's summer place.

A few years later, during the war, I remember she adopted her baby, Joanna, and then rented another apartment next to her beauty shop, so that Joanna would be brought up in a proper home.

I remember when she had a dress shop in St. Johnsbury, and many years later I realized what an ambitious, jostling businesswoman she was. When women started getting MBAs in the 1980s, I was reminded of my aunt Muriel. She would have been first in line to sign up for an MBA degree, but in the 1920s, and 1930s, when she viewed her business options, women could choose cooking or curling (usually in their homes), and she chose curling.

By the time I moved back to Vermont in 1963, Aunt Muriel had moved back from St. Johnsbury to live in my grandmother's house, where she started her Hardwick "Muriel Beauty Shop and Antiques" business. She had long since given up Slayton hounds, and moved on to Scotties. No matter how much she loved her dog, her idea of training was to use a flyswatter for unacceptable behavior. It always reminded me of my grandmother's "We'd better stop the car and get a switch, for the noisy children in the back seat."

My first year back in Vermont, when Bill and I stopped by her house during Christmas, I was aghast to learn that no balsam for her, as my dad and grandfather proclaimed that all Vermonters had to have for their Christmas tree. Oh no, tradition be hanged, she chose a long-needled pine tree! Yikes! Pine is not the smell of Christmas in Vermont! Balsam is.

A cigarette and black coffee were her sustenance all the years I knew her. Not one to eat much, the family told that she was a fat teenager and vowed never to be fat again. I think of her drinking very strong coffee, and according to Aunt Muriel, everyone else's coffee was "like dishwater." Joanna, Mary, and John, her daughter, niece, and nephew, remember her culinary skills by the doughnuts and filled cookies she made. I saw others eating them, but seldom saw Aunt Muriel ever take a bite.

No one could get what she wanted fast enough for her. Hitched to her oxygen machine at 85 years old, she asked me to find her violin and computer teachers. She had always wanted to play the violin, and she wanted to know what the excitement about computers was all about. I told her I would ask Susan at the *Hardwick Gazette*, to find two teachers for her. A day later she called me several times to demand, "Where are those teachers you said you would get me?" "Susan is looking for someone, she has called several people, but remember she has a fulltime job at the *Gazette*, a husband, and a pre-school boy to take care of. She'll call you when she finds the teachers." Impatient is an understatement to describe Aunt Muriel.

She had a way of taking the wind out of your sails. She would send me off balance faster than anyone I know. Her last "go" at me occurred when visiting her in the hospital, her last week of life. I disagreed with a plan that she had. She waited a moment . . . looked up at me from her bed and said, "What's so great about those little white earrings you've got on?" My hand shot up to my ear, wondering what I had on, as I stood there defending my very ordinary white earrings, completely forgetting my point of disagreement.

The last visit I had in her home was Monday, July 14th, the day I came back from Maine with a lobster for my Aunt Muriel. Although our family loves lobster, no one loved them more than she. Taking my picnic basket, wrapped lobster salad sandwiches, antique plates, black olives, pickles, chips, carrot cake, linen napkins, and stemmed glasses, I sat at her feet on a footstool. Falla, her dog, was sent to the kitchen, and she said with heavy breathing, but great relish, "A picnic at home . . . this is a first . . . and I love firsts!"

I stood looking at her after she died, and I thought of those words. I could just see her as she left this life for the next. Stepping curiously, with confidence, to greet the saints with, "HELLO! I'm Muriel and I love firsts . . ."

I Remember

∾

OUTDOOR SPORTS
IN HARDWICK

The mohawks. That's the name of the club that I hiked with in the snow on Sunday afternoons in the early 1940s. I never remember hearing that name before, but when talking to Burt Stone, Hardwick Trust Co., the summer before he died (1995), he informed me that I was a member of the Mohawk Club, which probably started in 1942. Burt and I went on to talk about the Mohawks as well as other outdoor sports in Hardwick.

The Mohawks met across from the Memorial Building after everyone had gone to church, had a big Sunday dinner with their families, and were ready for some Sunday afternoon exercise. Florence Lane

(Judge Taylor's daughter), Will Johnson, and Bill Robb (both Post Office workers), were the adults in charge on those beautiful Sunday afternoons. Floyd James, Floyd Bingham, and Burt Stone, Jr. were usually part of the Sunday afternoon group, according to Burt. I don't remember going with anyone my own age. All ages always did everything together in Hardwick. One advantage of small village life was that there were never enough people to discriminate against girls or children—Hardwick needed us all.

I wore the wool jacket my mother had made me with a wool hat that tied under my chin in order to use the attached hood to carry my lunch in the days before backpacks. We didn't have separate downhill and cross-country skis in those days, just one pair that we adjusted our made-up jar-rubber bindings to hike, or to ski downhill or to ski jump. The Mohawks met with some of us on snowshoes and others on skis. I remember Bill Robb and Will Johnson leading the way up Bridgman Hill, and just before we reached the reservoir, we took a right and went into the woods. Deep snow with fox, rabbit, and deer tracks were the only other signs of life. After a couple of hours of skiing or snowshoeing, we stopped, a bonfire was built on pine or spruce branches on top of the snow, and a pot of milk put on the fire. Everyone got hot cocoa to drink and marshmallows to roast with the sandwich they brought. Sometimes we hiked to the top of Bridgman Hill and skied or snowshoed down by Ed Appolt's farm way down to Hardwick Lake, passing by the pest house and the slaughterhouse that edged Hardwick Lake. We came back by the railroad tracks until we got to the Sullivan House—where we had started.

Hardwick's children grew up cross-country skiing to Hardwick Lake and skiing on the hills and meadows all around Hardwick. From Cannon Mountain at one end of town to Bridgman Hill at the other. Pre-schoolers on West Church Street started skiing on the little slope in back of Everett Campbell's and the Norcross houses (later the houses where Roger Lecours and John Hall lived), and then we graduated to the old Chautauqua field at the end of West Church Street, owned by Everett Bridgman, our local landscape artist. We built ski jumps with piles of snow, sometimes putting a wooden barrel down to build the jump as high as we dared. Waxing our skis with our mother's canning paraffin, we took short, fast glides to get a running start on a steep pitch and shout out, "No poles!" as we took off to leap through the air, herringbone-stepping back up the trail to pack it down and make our run faster for one more jump.

And when we got to high school, the thrill of the ski trails on Cannon Mountain, with Hardwick's first and only rope tow in 1948 and 1949, was the best. Bill Robb was in on that, too. He was always one to be doing for Hardwick's youth, teaching us how to play the brasses in the town band, leading the Boy Scouts, and then being a founding father of the ski tow in Mackville, below Cannon Mountain. The rope tow was powered by an old car motor, new trails cut through the woods, young maple saplings separated one trail from the other, a warming hut was built where for a short time we could even buy hot cocoa. I remember skiing with friends Kay O'Malley and Clare Robb in our army surplus white canvas parkas in high style after the war and watching the dare-devil boys flying through the woods at our very own Hardwick ski area.

Hardwick always blocked off Congo Hill for kids to go sliding all winter long. No cars allowed, and no sand trucks to ruin the fast slide. By junior high school, we were interested in nighttime, outdoor recreation, and we often pulled a traverse up Bridgman or Slapp Hill for a long slide home or skied at the end of West Church Street on moonlit nights.

Even though I chose skiing over skating, skating rinks were always big in Hardwick. There were many more skaters than skiers. Sheila Spier (Johnson) and many other kids' fathers even flooded their gardens and made their own skating rinks where we played hockey. Some village rinks had lights and music and a warming hut with a wood-burning fire. I remember the one above the Academy, and both Burt Stone and Harold Nunn remembered two others—the Spring Street skating rink in the late 1920s, and the rink of the 1930s at Ambrosini's field, supervised by recreation leader Shorty Tucker from Chelsea. Burt said that the Spring Street skating rink had a strict 9:00 p.m. curfew for children and teenagers, and then the adults used the ice rink after 9 p.m. Harold remembers the "boys" putting a stick of dynamite in the wood stove at the Ambrosini rink, and it burned rather than blew up as the fire wasn't hot enough to ignite it.

Speaking of recreation leaders, it would be impossible to talk about Hardwick's recreation programs without citing the program that Clara Travers started and ran from 1936 until 1943. Bobby Jones worked as her assistant from the beginning, until he joined the Air Force in 1941. It was a federally sponsored recreation program, the National Youth Administration (NYA), held in the Methodist Church on Church Street, later burned down by an arsonist where the Masonic Temple now stands. The most beautiful church of all, with the clock-face looking out in all four directions over Hardwick. I remember Clara's nursery school for three- to five-year-olds, and going to all the wonderful activities, with snacks of tomato juice and graham crackers that Aileen Parks (Moodie) and Clara planned for Hardwick's children. In the summer we had games of bowling, horseshoes, quoits, and a sandbox.

Clara remembers well her worry about the magnificent stained-glass windows, glass doors, and partitions when bowling balls and pins went flying through the air. Her solution was to build a chicken coop over the bowling alley; the pins hit the chicken wire then knocked over the other pins—quite a different game in a chicken coop! She laughs now to think of her courage around those beautiful church windows—and not one broken in five years! Besides the children's program that she ran, Clara was the Girl Scout leader for teenage girls—she organized cookouts, mountain climbs, ski hikes, camping and swimming trips.

The youth program was always short of money, Clara remembers. Recreation did not have a line in the Town or Village budget in those days. Fundraising was a major concern for the director. She often put on a puppet show and charged ten cents and a chunk of wood for the wood-burning stove that heated the church. Billy Lane, who lived right across the street, made many of the puppets and he was always there ready to organize the puppet shows and to help out for many money-making schemes.

Father Miller, pastor at the Episcopal Church, and Principal Erwin Hoxie were among the strongest supporters of the center. Perly Shattuck, Town Clerk and Treasurer, could see the children from his office in the Memorial Building. He kept a watchful eye out to see that things ran smoothly, and that Clara wasn't out there shoveling all the snow by herself. Anything connected with children, teenage girls, the outdoors, recreation, and good health—Clara Travers was always there, providing the leadership.

I asked Burt about the golf club that I remembered along the Greensboro brook before it runs into the Lamoille River that became Fisher's Nursery and Greenhouse. Burt replied that Hardwick had two other golf courses way before that one. The earliest golf course, about the time of the First World War, was on the top of Slapp Hill. The second and most successful golf course that lasted through the 1920s was on Bridgeman Hill. It was a 9-hole course in a cow pasture, the greens were fenced off (Fisher's golf course never had cows), and it was probably started by Ed Appolt, as he owed the farm up there (now the Shepard land in Vermont Land Trust). Burt gave me a list of those early members from the 1920s, which included his dad, Burt Stone, Sr., Jack Hall, Oscar Shepard, Waldo Bemis, Fosco Ambrosini, Taylor Holmes, Freddie Shattuck, Lewis Shattuck,

Clayton Clough, Alex McWilliams, George Ward, Lynn Wheeler, Floyd James, Floyd Bingham, and Wilbur Bingham. I had never heard of the two hill golf courses, but then, it's hard enough to admit to remembering the late 1930s. I do remember my dad taking me along in 1938. I walked the nine holes along the brook with him on Sunday afternoons. He wore his white linen golfing knickers, carrying the clubs that usually hung in the barn the rest of the week. According to Burt, "That was Hardwick's third golf course, and Ed Appolt's crowd became the new golf club down on the brook until WWII started."

Outdoors in Hardwick. Other than hunting and fishing and ball games, skiing, skating, sliding, snow-shoeing, and golf were certainly the big ones. Well, maybe some men would name horseshoes. There was a regular group down in back of the Houghton house, next to the Lamoille, where men had their horse-shoe teams. And for those of us who took part in those programs and grew up with so many other parents and adults looking out for us, we know now that we were blessed with a caring and safe community. In Hardwick, the village where we took our first steps out of our own families into the community. Many of us look back in wonder and thanksgiving for growing up in Hardwick's outdoors.

I Remember

❧

JENNIE ROWELL

February 14, 1986
Dear Bub, Anne, and Billy:

The first thing I remember about Jennie is that she was the only grown-up woman in Hardwick that I ever saw ride a bicycle. And she often rode it to the library. And I must not have been more than 5 or 6 and wondered why my mother didn't ride a bike, too.

And she was the only married woman in Hardwick that I didn't call "Mrs." because she told me I could call her "Aunt Jennie," and Mr. Rowell, "Uncle Bub." All the children on Church Street called the women, Mrs. Warren, Mrs. Hall, Mrs. Slayton, Mrs. Ladd, and for me—one "Aunt Jennie."

I remember the colorful 1940s dishes the Rowells had on the breakfast table, "Fiesta" orange, blue, cream dinner plates, cups and saucers. And when I'd run over and it was breakfast time, Jennie would have a high stack of toast in the middle of the table, loaded with butter, and how fast she would eat that toast and gulp down her coffee in great big gulps, her legs entwined below the table, sitting on the edge of the breakfast bench, ready to jump at any minute.

I remember her chocolate cake was a lot different than my mother's chocolate cake. And her cucumber and sunshine pickles were different than my mother's pickles, and her chip-beef gravy over boiled potatoes or saltines was just the same.

I remember sitting on the high stool, beside that table, and talking with Jennie as a grade schoolgirl, as an adolescent, and as a college student. I remember that she always took my side in everything. When I was in trouble with my family, when my dad said I couldn't go to the basketball game or to a school dance with a boy too old for me, Jennie would act like they didn't understand . . . and of course I was right! I remember Jennie always liking me and caring about me and taking me seriously at every age.

I remember how she used to vacuum the house every single day. I never saw anyone run through and do anything as fast as Jennie, and how she'd mop and wax that kitchen floor! And the accounts that she kept. Some Women's Studies historical societies should have her records! She knew the price of a can of peas in 1936, 1938, and 1948.

When I went away to college, I remember her letters always signed, "Best love." No one else I've ever met signed their letters that way. Learning since how imperfect even love can be, isn't "best" love the most caring thought possible to send?

And the last thing I remember about Jennie is when she stood in my mother's kitchen; I was in the middle of chemotherapy in NYC and had heard that Jennie was suffering memory loss and having a very hard time. I wanted to be sure and see her on this trip to Vermont. She arrived with Bub and didn't appear to recognize me. I watched her as she drank some juice after Bub telling her exactly how to do it. She was as thin as anyone could be. She stood up, leaned way forward on her cane with both hands, and looked at me. Peered, really. Then she slowly looked away and toward my mother . . . and then back to me. I couldn't believe that there was my favorite neighbor, Jennie, and she had no idea who I was. Then she told Bub she was leaving and went out to sit in the car. I went out to the car, reached in and touched her hand and said, "Jennie, I'm so glad you came to Hardwick today, I loved seeing you." She took her hand and put it on top of mine and said, "I'm glad to see you, too. You've really been through it, haven't you Joycie." Jennie was a sense of wonder to me from the first through the last memory I have of her. I love her very much.

Best love,

Joyce

I Remember

❦

COX'S SODA FOUNTAIN

KNOWN as Cox's Drugstore, most of us didn't have the pharmacist in mind or even Mr. Fournier, the watch repairman who worked by the big Grandfather clock in the window. No. The door opened most often for Helen's soda fountain—a long marble counter to the left of the door as we walked in—long enough for at least six high, leather-covered stools where high school girls sat. The two high stools, backs to the big windows on Main Street were where the men or boys always sat. Bill Robb always stood.

Cox's soda fountain was very different than other town's soda fountains because we never had hot chocolate for sundaes, just plain cold Hershey syrup in a can. And we never had walnuts on the sundaes like Parker's in St. Johnsbury or Bly's in Newport. We always had chopped peanuts. No banana splits in Hardwick. So—whenever I had a sundae anywhere else, it never tasted quite right with their hot chocolate and walnuts and a cherry or whipped cream on top.

I knew all the regulars at the soda fountain. I remember my best friend Sarah always had chocolate ice cream with butterscotch sauce. That was good. I seldom had a sundae, and I never had an ice cream soda or a milkshake because I didn't like things too sweet and besides, I didn't like to part with my hard-earned money. In high school, my favorite "after basketball practice" was a five-cent lemon-coke. Sometimes, not often, but for a special treat I bought a 10-cent package of Nabs. They sat in a little blue box right on the corner of the counter as I walked in. Two flavors were in that box. I could have had chocolate Oreos, but I always chose the peanut butter and cheese. Everyone had their own place—two down from the door where I could study the Nabs—on the long side of the counter.

Our iceman, Bub Rowell, who later became the Idle Hour Theatre owner and then Hardwick's Town Manager, was a "regular" and sat at the end of the counter at the window and always ordered a chocolate milkshake. I don't know if he ever had more than one, but I do know he had a chocolate milkshake every single day. Along with Bub Rowell, Bill Robb was also a regular. He worked at the Post Office and was my best friend Clare's dad. Besides that, he taught all of us kids who wanted to play in the town band how to play the brasses. He played the trumpet, his oldest son and his daughter Clare and I played the trumpet because he was the leader of the band and wanted a strong brass section for our parades in Hardwick—as well as in Albany, and Craftsbury. Mr. Robb went to Cox's every single day he was upstreet and ordered an Alka Seltzer. He never sat down. He just stood at the counter corner by that blue box of Nabs and drank his medicine.

And high school student Doris Barcomb, daughter of the Plymouth dealer (you may remember that the author was the daughter of the FORD dealer), sat on the end seat nearest the door and always ordered a sundae and sometimes a coke and Nabs to go with it. I secretly admired and was kind of jealous of her for being able to spend that much money all at once. My best friends, Sarah, Clare, and Kay didn't buy any more than I did when we were at Cox's soda fountain. They always had a cherry-coke. No Nabs.

O yes! The funny books were on a wall rack that could be reached by the two stools at the end of the counter. Roscoe, Jack, and Freddy, my classmates, would often sit there reading the comics until Helen would ask them to "Buy the funny book or put it back." I never saw one of them ever buy a funny book.

Cheerful Helen tended the fountain all the time I was in school. She was Hardwick's only single parent I had ever heard of. Cox's never was the same when for some reason she showed up one day working at the other drugstore in town, Irene Ashley's. That soda fountain is gone now. The whole building is gone. I don't even know when it was burned down. But I do know that if Cox's Drug Store were still there, it would smell just as familiar as it always did. And remembering the soda fountain, it's easy to imagine Bub sliding up on the corner stool while Helen reaches for the fixings of his chocolate milkshake. Cox's Drugstore is one of those Landmark Memories that comforts one's soul whenever a lemon-coke and peanut butter cheese Nabs come together. Cox's Drug Store ... the standard of excellence for all drugstores forever more.

I Remember

❧

HARDWICK ACADEMY

Hurrying to school up Main Street past Cox's Drug store and the Swinging Bridge, keeping the snow-covered Buffalo Mountain in sight on a cold winter's morning, finally pulling open the heavy door, feeling the heat rush toward me from the wood-burning, furnaced building, smelling the oiled wooden floors and seeing Mr. Bradford in the corner by the door as he pulled the rope to ring the last bell, are the first thoughts in my memory of Hardwick Academy.

Our elementary school teachers were all women we grew up with from Hardwick families: Miss Kneeland, Mrs. Robb, Miss Anair, Miss Warren, Miss Morgan. True, Miss Demars was from Greensboro, and Miss Parrott was from "away," but for the most part, our first Hardwick Academy teachers were no strangers to us. Mr. Jenkins was the Superintendent and by the time we got to the 4th grade, we had learned who was boss at H.A.

Organized in 1860, Hardwick's Opera House (Town House) was built to house the South Hardwick Academy in 1861. The second Hardwick Academy was built in 1893—the floors and stairs were well worn by the '40s. The annex was added in 1903 for 3rd and 4th graders downstairs and for 7th and 8th graders upstairs. The graduation class of 1907 came from Hardwick and East Hardwick, and from Albany, Cabot, Calais, Elmore, Greensboro, Lincoln, and Wolcott. There were 66 scholars in the Academy in 1907, and 441 students in the Graded School. The budget was $8,226.75 per-pupil—a high cost—documenting a community that valued education and a free library. The trustees at the time were familiar Hardwick names: H.R. Kimball, A.W. Norcross, and S.E. Darling. The school board also reported, "There are five churches in Hardwick and while attendance is not compulsory, it is greatly desired that all students will regularly attend at least the morning service of one of the churches."

The scariest and worst part of school for a first-grader was going to the basement. Do you remember lining up in a girls' or boys' line to go down those steep, dark stairs to the double row of grey-painted, wooden-wainscoting stalls, with sinks lined up on one side and open, dark, empty spaces on the other?

I can remember never going "to the basement" except for those times before or after recess when our teachers marched us down there. They stood by the sinks as we took turns and had to wait for the whole class before we could scurry back up those dark, steep stairs and into clean smells and light.

Remember the high ramp from the 7th and 8th grades that went out in back toward Cannon Mt.? Way up on top? Where the air-raid wardens used to stand trying to spot enemy planes during the war? From that place where we could ski down to Mackville? And where our only level playing field was for softball, baseball, and soccer? Like our neighboring schools in Greensboro, Hyde Park, and Craftsbury, we had one wooden structure with the first six grades downstairs and the next six upstairs. I never remember ever going upstairs during my first six years at H.A.

"Going upstairs," in the 7th grade was exciting, even if we were in the back of the building. Meeting Mrs. Mosher, our new English teacher who read to us every day right after dinner was wonderful. Johnny Thorp, the postmaster from South Woodbury, our first male teacher, was a new experience for all of us. We were more concerned about his country accent, his gender, and how he kept the hair out of his eyes than we were about what he was teaching. As 6th graders we were told that he used a paper clip to hold back his hair, and we were disappointed when we never saw that sight.

Hardwick had so few new people moving into town that it's easy to remember that Clark Hamilton and John Hanford joined our class in 4th and 5th grades, and Mike Case moved to Hardwick in 8th grade. Once here, no one ever seemed to leave except for teachers' or preachers' kids who weren't from Hardwick in the first place.

You could smell the muffins baking from the first door on the right at the top of the stairs of the second floor, where Miss Slayton taught young women the required three years of Home Economics. But the boys got to meander outdoors to the aggie classes and wear their blue FFA (Future Farmers of America) jackets. Mrs. Cobb, our 9th grade homeroom teacher, was the second on the right. Across from these classrooms were the study hall and library. I never remember using the library except for the dictionary, which was kept in the back, right-hand corner of the study hall, beside the pencil sharpener. The front of the room had a platform where the study hall teacher sat, catching us as we wrote and passed notes to each other. Mr. Mosher, our principal, had his office in the front center of the building—right under the bell tower. He was seldom there because he also taught junior and senior English and coached the girls' basketball team.

Unlike Greensboro and Hyde Park, H.A. didn't have a gym on the third floor. Being the biggest village around with the largest school, our third floor was used for classrooms, business education, and a chemistry lab. We could smell the Bunsen burners and chemicals of the chem lab where Mr. Woodcock's experiment stations lined the counter at the last room on the right. It was the only course with a poster on the wall that we were required to memorize. The first two doors on the right, however, were Mrs. Gile's domain. She was in charge of a complete business education in secretarial, accounting, and bookkeeping curriculums. Serious graduates of the business program could, and, often did, go straight into good jobs in Montpelier with the State of Vermont or National Life Insurance.

And the Wick room, our student newspaper was on the third floor in the belfry. Directly above the principal's office and below Mr. Bradford's bell that rang us to school each day. The student staff met in our belfry office to plan our stories and news, and I never remember a faculty member being there with us. The ladder to the Belfry was part of our office, just below the bell and where the older kids sneaked up for a smoke.

No one living in Hardwick in 1940 will ever forget the excitement of the beautiful new gym that was built for the Academy. Nobody anywhere had a gym like ours. Even our great rival, People's Academy, in Morrisville, who had all that Copley money for their school, had a sunken basketball court built from original plans of a swimming pool. Regular gym classes for all junior and senior students were required, and basketball was our first love. The basketball court was scheduled for girls' practice at 3, boys at 5, and town team at 7, five times a week from October through St. Patrick's Day when we had a special invitational basketball tournament to stretch the season out even longer. Mr. Mosher coached the girls in competitive basketball and Mr. Beardsley was the boys' coach. In fact, when I got to college and went out for basketball, at 5 feet tall, after the first few sessions, the woman's coach came over to me and asked, "Were you coached by a man in high school?" I was the only Vermonter and rural student and the fastest moving player in that group.

Sports varied from year to year as coaches and interests varied—there was a soccer team in 1932 because a coach came to Hardwick from Springfield College: Jim Gunn, who started soccer in Vermont schools, according to Burt Stone. Burt played goalie in 1933 and '34. There was always basketball for everybody and baseball for the boys—regardless of who was coach or principal or on the school board. The baseball field was up on the old circus grounds where Hazen Union now stands, Purple and Gold were our colors, the Terrier our mascot.

Once into our new gym we had one-act plays on our stage with the beautiful dark red velvet curtain, and an annual 3-act play, usually directed by the English teacher. Talent shows rounded off our drama education. We had a town band—our school being too small for a school band.

Buster Stevens, Rodney Storey, Billy Robb, Clare Robb, and I all played the trumpet. Sheila Spier played the trombone. And trombone player—Earl Wilson, Craftsbury farmer, was always first in Hardwick's marching band, with his trombone and his tall, long strides. Kathleen O'Malley and Marjorie Davis played the clarinet along with Will Johnson, Postmaster.

We had it all—especially considering that our high school had less than 100 students. No one had to be a talented actor or musician or athlete to make the team—everybody was needed. You don't know

how to play the clarinet or trumpet? That's OK—
bandleader Bill Robb taught us the brasses, and Will
Johnson taught the reeds. Both Post Office men volunteered their leadership for the sake of Hardwick's
young people. And music. And Hardwick. And
Memorial Day and 4th of July parades in Hardwick,
Craftsbury, and Albany. You don't have an instrument? That's OK, too. Someone will find something
to play—my trumpet came from the town librarian
Mrs. Hooper's attic.

Our choral music at school included a spring concert bringing together the glee clubs from Craftsbury
and Greensboro, under the direction of Mrs. Hoxie,
Hardwick's music teacher and wife of our superintendent. We always had a Christmas and Easter concert.
Hardwick girls swooned over Craftsbury Academy's
Morris Rowell, when he sang tenor solo for "Oh
Holy Night." In the Spring Concert we often sang
music from Broadway Musicals. I remember our
vigorous singing of "June is Bursting Out All Over,"
from Carousel.

Outside of sports, and drama and music, the Junior
Prom was the next biggest Hardwick Academy event.
In those days before TV, every H.A. event was a
town event. There wouldn't have been enough kids to
pay for the dance band so everyone from 7th graders
to our parents and grandparents came to the Junior

Prom. Fathers danced with daughters, mothers with sons; Mrs. Sullivan and other older women alone in town with or without children bought a ticket and sat along the wall watching the grand formal event. Juniors selected a theme, sent away for a complete decoration kit with crepe paper and logos and banners; we borrowed card tables from all over town, and students and parents made reservations for the tables. The new gym was transformed . . . lights were low, the music was sweet, the prom was wonderful. In 7th grade, my best friends Kay and Clare were too young to have dates, so my brother Jay took all three of us. We four reserved our card table for our very first Hardwick Academy Junior Prom. When we got to be juniors, our theme was "Under the Sea;" we decorated with fish and fish nets all around the place. I remember when Johnny Hall and Lorraine Charland, by far the most handsome and romantic couple at H.A., were crowned King and Queen at the Prom. In our junior year, Clare Robb was crowned Queen of the prom. The best big-band around was Guy Dunbar, who lived between Hardwick and St. J. His "Deep Purple," and "Good Night Ladies" were memorable. In those days most of us owned one or two formal gowns, and we wore the same one all through high school and college. Every one of us received a corsage from our date, all ordered and picked up by our date from the Holcomb Funeral Home. We had ballroom dancing lessons in 5th and 6th grade, so we knew how to waltz, foxtrot, and polka.

Very, very sadly, a tragic fire in 1959 brought Hardwick's beloved gym to the ground.

Proms, basketball, marching band—were there any academics to remember? English was without a doubt H.A.'s strength, with Mrs. Cobb getting us started in freshman and sophomore years. Besides our grammar lessons and learning all the parts of a sentence, we read and studied two Shakespeare plays, plus *Silas Mariner*, *Evangeline*, and the *Ancient Mariner*, in those two years. This was followed by Mr. Mosher, our principal and English teacher for grades 11 and 12. He was known for loving Shakespeare and requiring a lot of essays. He also introduced us to the major poets. I remember that Emily Dickinson was his favorite. In fact, the requirements of the "English Scientific" curriculum hadn't changed much from the required reading of 1907 at Hardwick Academy. Except in those days, students read all of the above plus *Pilgrim's Progress*. I don't think they spent as much time as we did on basketball! Although at the turn of the 20th Century, Hardwick Academy also offered the "Greek Scientific" and "Latin Scientific" curriculum. One of the first academic requirements we ever heard about when we got upstairs, is that the juniors and seniors had to write an essay every week.

Hardwick Academy. The last graduating class was in 1970, and the beautiful old building was torn down. I never remember going back into the school after graduation. But I live with H.A. every day, with Hazel Rochester's paintings of it in my home. All of Hardwick Academy's graduates live with their heritage in a time when school was equal to our home. The Purple and the Gold. It's odd to have been to a school that is no longer physically there. Nor is the name or our colors, mascot, and songs are gone forever. Did we ever hold a proper memorial service for Hardwick Academy? Let's lift our hearts and voices now in praise and remembrance, and join in one more last chorus of old H.A.'s grand alma mater:

Hail to thee, O Alma Mater
With your praises tell;
Glory to those who keep her,
Hail to thee, oh hail.

Loyal are we to our school,
And our colors, true;
They're the purple and the gold,
Glorious to view.

Far about the busy humming,
O'er the bustling town.
Reared against the arch of Heaven
Looks she proudly down.

I Remember

❧

HAZEL HALL ROCHESTER

H AZEL was my aunt Eunice's best friend since their Hardwick Academy days. Other H.A. classmates living in Hardwick during the '30s and '40s and still here in the 1960s were Ava Peck, community nurse, Burt Stone and Carroll Rowell, both local bankers, and Mercedes of Mer-Lu's Restaurant. They were all together in Hazel's oiling painting class in the 1960s.

Hazel was funny. Always in an ol' Vermonter kind of way . . . and with reason. She was a 5th generation Vermonter. Her father, Guy Hall, was a big guy with a funny eye, in coveralls and usually with his sidekick near-by, Arthur Austin, who took care of the gas pumps. Arthur was a little guy with one arm. The pair of them together were memorable—the big guy with one funny eye and the little guy with one arm.

Guy Hall, inventor. He had a blacksmith's forge and hammers in his metal shop where he could make any part anyone ever wanted. I sometimes went with my father and watched Guy Hall create parts in that red-hot forge, sparks flying, burning red hammers hammering for a Ford tractor, car, or truck part that wasn't being made during the war.

Hazel's mother, Ada Kimball, was a violinist, a tiny, soft-spoken woman. She was the only wife I knew who had a husband who would sit and listen to his wife read classical poetry and literature together in the evenings. Well, maybe the Cobbs?

My grandfather and father both said that the Halls were Hardwick's Communists. That was because the Halls were Democrats and the only ones I ever heard of.

Guy Hall's daughter Hazel was tall and political, like her dad. Unlike her father, Hazel was very beautiful. She spent only one year at Vermont's University, UVM.

Well, it didn't take long before a senior at UVM's Medical School fell in love with Hazel, her very first year away from Hardwick. Those were war years. When couples met, fell in love quickly, married, and separated often. Hazel's new husband was sent on an overseas mission and so Hazel made the best of her opportunity to study painting at Pratt Institute and the Art Students League in New York City. Next thing we knew, she was on her way back to Hardwick with two young children and no husband to live in the house next door to her parents. Creating a studio in that big, old, classical Hardwick home was Hazel's first job. Quickly and so well done.

Oh, so talented . . . and so creative . . . and so hard working just like her parents' lifestyle. Hazel supported her family with her designs and craftsmanship of silk-screened Christmas cards, followed by a line of enamel-on-copper jewelry, that she sold all over the USA. Her studio quickly filled with lamps, pendants, and oil paintings—with scenes of Hardwick's landmark buildings and landmark people.

And oh, so political. Hazel chose her buildings to paint as her preservation effort to save Hardwick's landmark buildings. More than leaving Hardwick an oil copy, Hazel went over to our capital, Montpelier, to rally against the demolition of each of those buildings. She painted the Eagle Hotel and the Hardwick Inn, Swinging Bridge, Idle Hour Theatre, Hardwick Academy, and Main street. She often added Hardwick's characters who appeared only on Saturday nights, as well as those she saw downstreet or coming and going by foot, pick-up or horse and wagon.

When I moved back to Vermont with my new husband and we lived on a farm nearby in Wolcott, I stayed home with our two children and wrote books. And how I loved going by Hazel's studio to see what she was working on, and to hear her latest political rant and rave in the world. If my Aunt Eunice was there, I'd be assured of good Scotch and loads of their '30s and '40s sultry stories and jokes.

Whenever I went down to New York City to sell a book idea, I'd come back home with an advance in my pocket. The only "extra" I bought with the money was a Hazel Hall Rochester oil painting. Every time I sold a book, I bought a painting. I remember Hazel's words to me, after buying about a half-dozen paintings, oh so typical of her humor and word imagery: "Why, you've got more ideas spewing out of you than puke out of a puppy!"

Main Street by Hazel Hall Rochester.

Hardwick Academy by Hazel Hall Rochester.

Hardwick Inn by Hazel Hall Rochester.

Jeudevine Library. Painting by David Olson.

I Remember

❧

SLAYTON MOTOR SALES

My Father's Garage

I MUST have been about a third grader when I had my first lesson in labor and management. My father never went "down to the garage" after supper. But this night he asked if I wanted to ride down with him, as he had to settle a strike with the mechanics. Even though I had no idea what that meant, I could tell it was serious.

I sat in the dark car, even so, could clearly see through the large front office window the conversation with his two mechanics, Cecil Robarge and Fletcher Potter. I say conversation. More like watching a stage play of three standing men, under bright lights saying one-liners, acting their nods and pauses, and smoking—finding the pack, lighting, inhaling, exhaling, flicking ashes, grinding butts.

I noticed at first glance the difference between work clothes of ankle-high work shoes, short jackets, and caps, and management clothes of white shirt and tie, felt hat and long coat. I thought that handsome Cecil Robarge looked like Clark Gable with his mustache (not seen often in the early '40s) and beret, probably the only beret in Hardwick.

They weren't on stage for long. The two men turned and walked out, and my dad turned off the light and was soon back in the car, driving home. The strike was over. The mechanics got a raise, although I wouldn't have known it by the expressions on any of their faces. But I did know that my father's mood was more relaxed on the ride home. I asked how people would get their cars fixed if there were no mechanics working. Wrong question.

I remember Hardwick's Ford business before the tractors and farm machinery business, which started at the beginning of the war. I remember when, in elementary school, a car transport rumbled into Hardwick with a load of new Fords on it—easily as exciting as the circus coming to town. I can remember spotting one as I passed in front of the Eagle Hotel, took a left, and headed down Wolcott

Street to my father's garage. A couple of times I remember watching how the men unloaded the car from the transport. Even though there were a lot of cars on it—only one was left at Slayton Motor Sales—this little dealership in Hardwick, Vermont.

During the war, with car production almost stopped, the small dealers would usually, not always, get one car a month. A quota or allotment depended on the population of the area. Those war days were the days of rationed gas, a "governor" installed so you couldn't drive over 50 miles an hour, gas coupons, and people changing their driving and buying habits. Those who always bought a new car every year, or at least every other year, couldn't buy one until the war was over.

Walking into the showroom of my father's garage always smelled like new cars. The used trade-ins were in the yard, new cars were never left out in the sun. Whenever our family drove anywhere, we always had to park in the shade, because the "sun ruins the paint."

The parts department, managed by Bob Smith for all the years I remember going to the garage, was the most interesting place to be—shelves and racks of new parts, neatly lined up in graduating sizes. Bob stood at the parts counter pouring over the big picture books of each part. If he didn't have the part, someone would "skip" over to St. J. or Barre to get it. My mother liked to get that job.

Going to the right off the showroom, to the shop where the mechanics did the serious work, I always liked to look through the toolboxes that the mechanics owned. I'd watch them scoot under the cars on those little wooden trollies with tiny wheels, just like a modern-day full body skateboard. Next I went out to the "road to Burlington" side of the garage where Joe Smith did all the small stuff: grease jobs, lubes, pumping gas, inspections, and fixing flat tires. After the war, Leslie Ainsworth worked there, more or less as the body man, as the Slayton household always said, "Leslie fix!" Leslie was an inventor and like Hardwick's Guy Hall, he could fix anything and everything. If he didn't have the part, he made it.

Usually I started my tour of what's going on at the garage by going into the office, a two-room space. In the first room I always found my grandmother at her bookkeeping desk, window facing the showroom with the garage safe to her right. She sat at her desk entering all those bookkeeping figures and writing bills with her "Palmer Method" style of penmanship. Betty O'Malley did the same thing at Ted O'Malley's filling station upstreet. I never saw my grandmother move from her desk chair—she didn't seem as interested as I was in watching cars go up and down on the air lift, or the men scooting around on their backs under the cars.

Larry Sholan, tractor salesman and mechanic from 1942 until he was called into the war, often ambled over from the tractor building to liven up her day with his latest funny story. My grandmother drove her Model A Ford to work every morning, drove home for dinner at noon, sometimes coming to our house for dinner, and drove back home at closing. All business.

Bob Smith's desk was on the opposite wall, facing my father's office, although he was usually standing at the parts counter, or checking with "the boys" to see how they were coming along on the job, and then calling the customer about the progress. Anyone who wanted to talk to my grandmother or Bob, just stood there by the stove and talked, there wasn't a chair for anyone to sit down. I remember Urban Martin Sr. standing there talking to my grandmother about sugaring season (tapping the maple trees and boiling the sap to make syrup in March), which she always asked him about, no matter what time of year it was.

I waited for my father in his office, the second room. Sitting in his office with a metal ashtray filled with cigarette butts, it was clearly a man's world. I never saw a woman sitting there ordering a new car.

A bookshelf on one wall held the latest issues of the *Ford Times*, and sample books of upholstery choices for cars, slick booklets with photos of new cars, lots of convertibles and station wagons (known in the 1940s as Beach Wagons), another book of all the colors one could order.

I liked to sit in my father's swivel chair, and look through those books of style, color, and fabric. And if anyone called my house, I could pick up his phone. Six-nine-ring-two was home and six-nine-ring-three was the garage. If Kay or Clare called me, the operator knew I was at the garage and she rang up there. Of course I wasn't allowed to use the phone at home during the day, because it could tie up the business line.

I didn't work much for my dad. I remember one summer when I persuaded him to let me pump gas for a couple of weeks before I went to Camp Hochelaga (where I had to earn half of the cost in order to go). But I wasn't big enough to lift the hood to check the oil, or tall enough to reach over to wash the windshield (and I never did get tall enough). But I reasoned with my dad that it would save time if I pumped the gas while Joe Smith did the other stuff. Most people had a running tab for credit, and I liked writing the price on a credit tablet on a special wall desk after I pumped the gas.

Having a father in the car business was the most wonderful thing for a teenager. I could drive anything at any age around his yard: pick-ups, tractors, trucks. Once I had my license at 16, I wanted the Model A. During the war someone traded in a real WWII Jeep and that was my all-time favorite. Short-lived, however, as my father deemed it unsafe—no roof or roll bar. I'd get my friends in that Model A in the winter and slew around—making a perfect circle at the four corners by the Memorial Building and Library. That was the most fun. The same Model A was often stuck in the mud during April's mud season. Many times, Annette Rowell's father had to get his work horses out to pull my Model A out of the mud when I got to her farm—cussing at me the whole time.

Of course my dad taught me how to drive so I knew how to change a tire, to put on chains, and how to get out of a snow bank, out of the mud, and how to be a good driver. "Always expect the unexpected" my dad would constantly repeat as I learned to drive beside him. I never drive on a dirt road without his voice cautioning me to drive in "the middle of the road and if you bump to one side or the other, or if a deer jumps out into the road, you won't go off the road into the ditch." "A good driver doesn't use his brakes all the time, you look ahead and slow down by easing up on the gas pedal before you have to stop."

I used to practice driving to Morrisville (14 miles) without once using my brakes. And I knew by experience how to get the car out of a ditch. One of the earliest times I got a car to drive by myself, I was up at the music camp between Greensboro and Craftsbury, a very rough, washboard dirt road above Eligo Lake. I decided if I was old enough to drive a car, I was old enough to smoke. I bought a package of Pall Malls (not in Hardwick, of course, where the storekeeper would tell my father), those long cigarettes in a beautiful red package. While bumping along on that narrow, dirt, washboard road, I tried lighting my cigarette and bumped right off into a very deep ditch. No traffic going by up there. Nor was I going to walk away. No way I was going to call my father. I got out the bumper jack, jacked it up, pushed it over off the jack toward the road, repeated this process many, many times, until the Model A was finally in the road enough to drive away. Phew! I didn't give up smoking or driving, but I learned a lesson about paying attention when driving!

I remember as a college student coming home and saying something about my grandfather's garage. I clearly learned then, that my father hadn't been "given" his business on a silver platter. Oh no. I learned that though my grandfather had started the Ford business in Hardwick, he had lost it to the bank during the Great Depression. And in 1931, a newly married man with experience as a car salesman in Newport, where my father fell in love with my mother, he came to Hardwick and bought the business back from the bank.

Since growing up, I often thought the Ford business was an unlikely place for my father to be. He hated change. It took him a year to get used to the changes Ford proudly made to their new cars. And then, of course, it was time for the new cars with all of Ford's exciting modern features to come out. When the automatic transmission came out—that was the worst! When people were interested in style or color, he would explain to them that a "car is only for transportation." And remind them that Henry Ford told Ford dealers to give the people any color they wanted . . . as long as it was black. Instead of being enthusiastic about new design and improvements, such as automatic chokes, directional lights, and the dimmer moved from the floor to the wheel, he would say, "The more automatic things on a car there are, the more things there are to go wrong." When a new car customer brought his car back with a complaint, my father would respond with, "The old ones rattle and the new ones squeak." Marketing was not his thing.

Selling cars, trucks, tractors, and farm machinery were seldom on his mind. Hunting and fishing were. But my dad made the Ford business a good match as he could combine his work with his love of the brooks and deer stands to be found everywhere in Vermont's Northeast Kingdom. When my father started selling tractors, around 1941, our family sat down for supper at 5:30 sharp and we would be in the car by 6, driving the back roads in spring, summer, and fall to "call on a farmer." When we got there, my mother, Jay, and I sat in the car while my father stood and talked about hunting and fishing with the farmer. They would point to an apple orchard, look at the hounds, and talk about the coldness and purity of that trout brook. Cars, trucks, tractors and farm machinery were seldom mentioned. A week or even months later at the supper table, my dad would announce "so and so" came in to look at a tractor that day, the farmer we called on to talk about hunting.

Slayton Motor Sales was good, too, because my dad could always be fishing on the first day of May, the opening day for trout fishing. In the Ford business he could hunt every day until he got his deer, during the two-week November season, and go bobcat hunting when the February snow was high, and the crust just right for holding his weight with snowshoes and the dog.

My father sold the garage to Roger Slayton in 1964.

It turned out that Slayton Motor Sales was a good business for my dad. He always knew what he valued most. A quality life meant taking his family to the Ford Show in Montreal for French pastries, to Boston for Chinese food, and to New York City for hot pastrami sandwiches; hunting and fishing throughout each season. He always said he could work, "Just enough to pay for what he wanted to do." I remember my father's garage, Slayton Motor Sales, the little Ford dealership in Northern Vermont. The business that gave him what he valued most—time for hunting and fishing, as well as hunting the best in seasonal foods for his family.

Just before a Boston trip in the mid-1940s where he was taking me to see the Red Sox-Yankee game, my dad said to me, "America is a wonderful country—the little man can do anything a rich man can do and go anywhere a rich man can go—he just can't stay so long."

I Remember

◠

BURT'S AUCTION: THE REDISTRIBUTION OF HARDWICK'S TREASURERS

1. Buy only in best possible condition
2. Do not buy at auction unless examined beforehand
3. Know your subject—study
4. Beware of reproductions
5. Learn where to look for signatures and marks

O UR auction lesson for the day according to Burt Stone, Jr. (July 19-21, 1996), as read by auction-eer Duane Merrill, top auctioneer in Vermont, to introduce this extraordinary auction in Hardwick. Written in Burt's hand, these rules were found on a "Record of Inventory" in 1976. Oh! If only we could follow his advice. Even though I listened carefully, a couple of hours later my pride in winning a great bargain on a perfect "Gone With the Wind lamp," quickly turned to shame as I was handed a reproduction! I had not examined beforehand, studied my subject, nor bewared of reproductions . . . three of five of Burt's auction rules were broken, and the price was paid.

The excitement mounted all week, as Hardwick, Greensboro, and Craftsbury people talked of the forthcoming auction, Burt's auction—the social event of the season. Pam Crandall's fascinating *Hardwick Gazette* article, the Gazette listings of the auction, and the auction brochure all added to the hyperbole. On Thursday, July 18th, hundreds of viewers took seriously Burt's rule #2 and examined each piece at the Greensboro Inn (the Inn was sold before the auction to a young, ambitious, and visionary couple with Greensboro and construction business ties). Some came to the Inn to get an idea of treasures for sale; many others came because the viewing was the only game in town.

The bustle and excitement rose steadily early Friday morning until we were all in whatever seat we brought with us, spread out in a semi-circle around the auctioneer by 10:00 a.m., not to move again until 6:00 p.m. My auction neighbors settled in: John

Slayton, Allen Davis, the Lepine sisters (Jeannette and Gertrude from Mud City), Connie Shattuck Robb, and Pam Crandall within smiling distance. We were mesmerized by the extensive collection and sale of furniture (a Vermont-made pine bureau of the 1830s went for $800, a mahogany dining-room table brought $2,000); a 20" Hudson River model train engine sold for $600; important photographs (a rare Rodin sold for $13,500, the Steichen of Miss Jean W. Simpson bought at $1,100); braided and hooked rugs, $210; quilts went for $200, pine blanket chest for $300; the top bid for the John Elliot of Philadelphia mirror was $3,300. We Hardwickians nodded and winked at each other as we recognized that the summer people had different standards and means than we did—to buy these treasures.

But high prices for quality antique treasures don't begin to tell the story: Hardwick artists Bridgman and Rochester were neatly and quickly bought by folks born and raised in Hardwick. Jimmy Sholan got the album of Hardwick postcards he came after; Allen Davis was happy with his lithograph of the "Birdseye View of Hardwick" from the 1800s at $150, but happiest of all because he got to buy back a truck that Burt had bought at Allen's father's auction. Even though Pam Crandall was outbid on the Grueby pottery she coveted, she did get a Bridgman and a green porcelain lamp that took her eye. Speaking of buying back—we all applauded when Lucinda Rochester was high bidder for her mother's West End painting that she wanted at $675; Lewis Shattuck got the Hardwick Gazette building that his dad owned—in a Hazel Hall Rochester's "Swinging Bridge" painting for $595; Connie Shattuck Robb got Hazel's Methodist Church painting with the wonderful clock-face spire, and her childhood home next to it, for $500; and Miss Rowell from East Craftsbury recovered the many Jean Simpson water colors and monographed lines that Burt had bought at the Jean W. Simpson auction.

This writer won the bid at $350 for the Rochester "Roby Mill" and again for the "Black River Valley" with Jay Peak for her friend Parker Ladd (H.A. 1946). John Slayton bought a museum-quality silk braided tabletop rug as a surprise for his sister. The Lepine sisters ended up with $2,700 worth of Frank Wallace paintings, wood blocks, and drawings. Look for a Wallace retrospective in Stowe in the next year. They also bought every antique food chopper in sight—35 of them! Greensboro's Diane Irish loved the early flint-glass crystal as her Californian mother and Texas cousin couldn't resist the hooked rugs and sterling pieces. Hardwick antique dealer Dick Sullivan and other local antique dealers and even a NYC dealer were scattered around and cleaning up on the lots of silver, linens, frames, and Vermont memorabilia. The Cabot clock man was present.

Many a good buy was made at Burt's auction.

When the first day was over, a few of us gathered at Greensboro's Highland Lodge to swap auction stories of the day, and raise our glasses in memory of Burt Stone, Jr. Just as our glasses rose to our lips, the electricity dimmed, blinked, and went out for a moment. Standing in a circle, each of us looked up and bade our last farewell to Burt as he appeared to graciously give us a grand sign from above.

I Remember

❦

FIRST CONGREGATIONAL, EAST HARDWICK

IF I got close enough and concentrated enough, I could catch those alto notes that I longed to sing. The best surprise of going to church with my reclaimed summer friend, musician Pat Hall, was her voice. She can sing alto without any help. Once we started the hymn, I never looked up once to see how the new minister stood smiling out at all the Hardwick people during the hymns. As I tried intently to read the music and at the same time as getting the word to the second, third, and fourth verses, I listened with all my might in order to come in on a few of those notes. After about two verses of very quiet hard work, Pat leaned down to whisper,

"The Lord wants to hear a joyful noise, don't worry about the note!"

All summer long we sat in our own United Church of Hardwick place, greeting the families that we had grown up with. If I didn't recognize one or two of the congregation, I was certain that they knew me. After all, this was the church where I grew up and where I was married and my parents buried. So, there we were, coming to the end of the summer season and wanting to do more for our minister's summer church of faithfuls in nearby East Hardwick.

Announced and billed as a hymn sing, Pat and I decided to follow our summer Sunday service with a rural church experience in East Hardwick, just to see what it was like. We were curious because after all, we were kind of "summer people," even though we were born and brought up in Hardwick. I had left at 17 never to return, and she had left as a young widow as soon as her son had finished school. We convinced a soprano to join us, an "out-of-stater" who had moved to Hardwick this summer and who not only could sing, but had a trained, professional voice.

Arriving at the smallest church I have ever seen, I couldn't help thinking it must have been a one-room schoolhouse in the 1850s. The small, white clapboard structure was set back from the road against a stand of maples, birches, and spruces. I didn't recognize the woman with the walker, the woman with the baby, the three women sitting together. I did recognize the young man and his wife.

My first step inside the church took a minute to adjust to the light from this very bright, crisp, August day with white billowing clouds sailing in a deep blue sky. But more than light, I had to adjust my whole sense of being and timing as I took in the curved, worn pews leading to the front of the church. I saw a Victorian table which held a single candle, and a small, wooded cross on a stand. The scene felt like an authentic stage-set for an early 1940s Broadway show—a period piece, not a single item out of time. To the right was a recently refinished oak pipe organ with a high bench that looked as if it had been born there. And beside the organ, an upright piano in a dark finish. The Hardwick Librarian had been persuaded to be the organist at First Congregational, East Hardwick, and she slid along the organ bench, flipped the switch, and we could hear the motor warming up as she practiced a few chords.

At the same time, Hardwick's new minister and congregation started visiting informally with each other as if we were in someone's front room. The middle-age woman with the young husband was excited to learn that the new minister had been voted to be the pastor of the United Church of Hardwick.

Others talked about their Sunday dinner plans, picnic plans, taking a dinner to a shut-in plan, getting a 90-year-old into a van for a Sunday afternoon ride, and sharing garden vegetables during the week. A spirit of friendliness and neighborliness took over this tiny congregation. I wondered if Sunday morning in these caring environments always brought neighbors together to be so concerned for others. How could the table and photo and curtains and windows look so old? How could so little change have taken place in this congregation? How could the people of this church ring so true from another time dimension? Is it really 1990 in East Hardwick? Are there other little pockets of goodness, gentleness, and grace scattered around America? Around the rest of the world? I bet there are.

The new minister strode to the front in her Sunday dress, as the formality of a robe must have seemed like too much for this small congregation. She called us to worship and spoke briefly outlining this morning's service. We began with singing "Blessed Assurance," continuing with "The old Rugged Cross," "Bringing in the Sheaves," Amazing Grace," "Take Time to be Holy," and we even sang "Come to the Church in the Wildwood." Only the words, not the music, were printed in our booklets . . . disappointingly no struggle for the alto part in East Hardwick."

Years ago, 50 lets say, I remember hearing "Come to the Church in the Wildwood" every single Sunday morning on Waterbury's WDEV radio station. And here I stood reclaiming the comforting familiarity of a 1930s childhood in this East Hardwick Church.

After several hymns, selected randomly from our booklet by the congregation, a prayer was said and concerns of the church were discussed. At this time the new minister received well wishes for her acceptance as pastor and we three from the United Church of Hardwick were applauded for adding our welcomed voices to the hymn singing.

Next, we were asked to give generously as we are given to. Looking up to see how the collections were going to go, my eye was caught by the breeze parting the sheer curtains of the long, narrow, arched, clear glass windows, to catch a glimpse of the sparkling, green August day through the open window. Focusing back inside is when I spotted the oldest woman I've ever seen walking silently among us, passing the collection plate. I couldn't help but be reminded of the dramatic contrast to my Brick Presbyterian Church on Park Avenue in New York City where women aren't allowed to be ushers nor collectors of the money and where the smart, brisk men with pinstripe suits and a fresh white carnation in their buttonhole step ever so lively and efficiently to collect the offering.

We sang several more hymns, no one was looking at their watch or eager to leave, so we sang "just one more hymn" three times. As soon as the Benediction was pronounced, we three Hardwick guests were greeted and thanked and conversations began, "How I miss your mother," was said to me, and a young man said, "I remember you now, I used to mow your folks' lawn after you kids left Hardwick."

Walking reluctantly and slowly away . . . looking up into the heavens of that August blue sky, the drama of life—the ups and downs that each of us encounter, the strife and stress of the human condition—paraded before my eyes as I thought, *First Congregational East Hardwick has just provided me with a timeless and forever life experience of being thankful—no matter what.*

I Remember

༄

SALLY SLAYTON'S
RED RECIPE BOX

MARGARET GALLAGHER'S filled cookies: Margaret Gallagher's? She baked? It never crossed my ten-year-old mind that the dourest postal clerk in town had a life outside of the post office that included baking cookies. Or making or eating anything sweet.

I carefully looked at my mother's well-worn red recipe box that sat on the pantry shelf in our house, and now sits on my kitchen windowsill. The delicious Hardwick memories flood back. I had never noticed before that the faded, red recipe box, strapped with masking tape, was a Christmas gift from B.W. Hooker and Co., Barre, Vermont, 1931– the year my folks were married.

Here is Roscoe Cobb's rug cleaner recipe. And even though everyone made devil's food cake, Mrs. Ladd's recipe is the one in my mother's box. Mrs. Ladd came over for tea every single afternoon with my mother, before their husbands came home for a 5:30 sharp supper. I found her recipes for Kris Kringle Fruit Cake, Toll House Layer Cake, and Broiled Egg Plant? Strange, because I never remember seeing an eggplant before I left Vermont. How do I know these recipes were hers? Because I know Mrs. Ladd's handwriting. When an out-of-state friend asked how I knew the handwriting of Mrs. Ladd or Mrs. Cobb or Jennie Rowell, I quickly explained that Hardwick grown-ups always wrote to the young people when we went away to camp or college.

Mrs. Magoon's Chocolate Cup Cakes. That was the woman with a deaf daughter who moved to the Myrtie Thomas house during the war, on West Church Street. It was the first time any of us kids ever met a deaf kid.

And here is Fran Holcomb's Eagle Brand Date Bars, Sal Densmore's Spinach Salad with Lemon Jell-O, and Lucy Jenkins's Pin Wheel Cookies. Esther Albee's Russian Tea, also a punch base, because remember that Esther was always entertaining ever since she ran the Hardwick Inn. Look at this one! An "Overseas Fruitcake," 1945. And it doesn't have any fruit in it! It calls for "fat," vanilla, sugar, marmalade or jelly, eggs and flour. Oh yes, a cup of raisins. I wonder where the sugar came from?

Looking through the cookie section of the batter-splattered cards are Eva Bemis's Soft Spice Hermits. As little kids we all knew that Eva's mother, Mrs. Bardelli, did the cooking while Eva managed her 5 and 10 cent store. I bet those are Mrs. Bardelli's hermits.

My mother's neighbor across the fence, Mrs. Spier, was my mother's first friend who died. Here is Mrs. Spier's favorite recipe for:

Ruby's Gingerbread Waffles

½ cup shortening

¼ cup sour milk

2/3 cup brown sugar

2 cups flour

1 t. soda

2 eggs

1 t. baking powder

1 t. ginger

½ cup molasses

½ t. cinnamon

1/8 t. cloves

Hardwick homemakers were all such experienced cooks that you will notice that there are seldom any directions as to what to do with the ingredients.

It's hard to keep all the "White's" straight. First, there's Dot White's (now Gray, of course) Sour Cream Cookies and Walnut Meringue Bars made with Currant Jell-O, then here is Betty White's Pumpkin Bread. She was the minister's wife in the 1930s before John Chester Smith arrived in Hardwick. And of course, there were the Bob Whites of St. Albans (their champion basketball team was named "The Bob Whites") and here is Ruth White's Salmon and Cheese Casserole. Everyone in Vermont knew them because Bob was the best basketball coach up in St. Albans, who always came to Hardwick to hunt deer with my dad.

Speaking of the Whites reminds me of Mrs. Smith (now of East Hardwick). She was the first person I ever heard of who used oleo instead of butter (she was from New York, not a dairy state). And her good friend, Mrs. Cobb, has a corned beef recipe in the red box, along with her hermits. That doesn't seem right . . . I never saw Sarah or Roscoe eating anything except their father's brownies, and we all knew that Mrs. Cobb was best known only for her brown bread to go with their Saturday night Boston Baked Beans.

I wonder how many remember Art Bacon's barber shop next to the Idle Hour Theatre. That was before he moved further downstreet around the corner from Cox's Drugstore and across from the Hardwick Inn. Cecille Bacon gave my mother a recipe for Captain Casserole made with rice and tuna.

The only friend of my parents whom kids could call by their first names, but only because we called her "Aunt Jennie," was best known for her devil's food cake and sunshine pickles, but here is another good one:

Aunt Jennie's Maple Cottage Pudding
1 cup maple syrup (bring to boil)
1 T. shortening
3 T. sugar
1 egg and ½ cup milk
1 cup flour
1 t. baking powder
¼ t. salt

Cream shortening and sugar, add beaten egg, milk, flour. Stir well and add the maple syrup. Bake 25 minutes. Turn upside down on plate and sprinkle with nuts if you wish. Serve with whipped cream.

We always had a fresh pie for dinner and a pudding for supper, here is brother John's all-time favorite:

Grapenut Pudding

½ cup grapenuts
1 beaten egg
½ cup sugar
2 cups milk
Cook in double-boiler.

Even though my mother baked a pie every single day for dinner because my dad wouldn't eat day-old pie, she seldom made my grandmother's pie that is so rich you can eat only half a piece; except for my brother Jay, of course. Known to our family as:

The Dix Cream Pie

1 cup sugar
½ t. cinnamon
1 cup sweet cream
½ t. nutmeg
1. T flour
Dash of salt
¼ t. cloves

Mix sugar, flour, add cream. Pour over spices, cover with top crust and bake 30-40 minutes.

Every few years my mother thought she should make marmalade. This one was her favorite:

Rhubarb Marmalade

2 oranges and 1 lemon sliced and cut in small pieces—enough water to cover—cook until tender. Add little water if necessary when cooked—add 6 cups white sugar and about a quart of rhubarb cut into 1-inch pieces. Cook slowly until thickened.

If my father was not home for dinner, we ended up with Salmon Loaf. It seemed very much like Salmon Wiggle to me, except my father loved Salmon Wiggle and he never ate Salmon Loaf. But go ahead and try it . . . it's good!

Sally's Family Salmon Loaf

1 can red salmon (1 lb.)
2 T. minced onion
½ cup milk
½ t. salt (or omit)
½ cup soft bread crumbs
1/8 t. pepper
4 T. melted butter

3 egg whites stiffly beaten

3 eggs—4 yolks lightly beaten

juice of ½ lemon

Reserve liquid from can of salmon and flake salmon into bowl. Scald milk—add crumbs and butter, let stand 5 minutes. Add salmon liquid and beat smoothly, then combine with salmon, egg yolks, lemon juice, onion, pepper, and a green pepper diced, if you have one.

Fold in beaten egg whites. Bake at 350 for 35-40 minutes. Serve with white sauce.

These recipes were cooked and served in a different Hardwick age. The age of Bub Rowell, the friendliest ice man who gave us kids a chip of ice on a hot day; when Mr. Boudreau sold meat from the back of his little panel truck and sold kids a hot dog (raw, of course) for a penny; it was the age of Mr. Duby coming to Church St. by horse and sleigh (or wagon) to take orders and deliver them from the Davis store on the other side of town. The age when Henry Goodrich drove his horse down Bridgman Hill in his black canvas-topped carriage with round windows on each side to deliver butter. It sounds like hundreds of years ago ... but for Hardwick, that's the way we lived until after the war (WWII).

That Red Recipe Box is filled with better memories than tastes.

I Remember

∽

THE OLD GREEN
IRON BRIDGE

S o long, old green iron bridge. Let's see, I would
have walked over your sidewalk on the left-hand
side, going downstreet nine thousand, nine hundred
and sixty times just getting to school. That's 12 years
of school, 4 times a day, 185 days a year. Add the extra
bridge crossings to Hardwick Academy's basketball games, dances at the gym, Halloween parties,
and the total could easily swell to more than 10,000
crossings. How well did I know you? Ten thousand
crossings are a lot of knowing.

I remember the excitement of climbing up the end
of the divider and walking across the top between
the sidewalk and road. And sitting on that green
divider—about four feet high as all our parades

marched across the bridge. Every parade marched downstreet from above the Library and Memorial buildings and paraded up Main Street. That divider between walker and cars is etched in my mind with its gracefully rounded corners, its evenly spaced rivets—half an inch high, about the size of a quarter, or a half-dollar, even, edging the divider. Those rivets kept our feet from slipping as a 5- or 6-year-old first learned to climb up to walk the length of the bridge on top of the two dividers.

I remember extra bridge crossings from school. In first and second grade, when we marched double file, holding hands from school down the street, across the bridge, and up to the Opera House (currently called the Town Hall) for Memorial Day exercises, music concerts, and other school performances held there before we had a school gym. And crossing again to Jimmy's gym after Hardwick Academy's first gym burned down. I remember, too, marching two by two down Main Street, standing by the bridge for Memorial Day ceremonies during WWII. That's when the Hardwick American Legion tossed the memorial wreath into the river, taps were played, shots fired to commemorate our lost servicemen on that old green iron bridge.

As a third or fourth grader, sometimes I just stood still looking down through the gratings into the Lamoille. Standing there with my school pals, watching the river flow under us—watching, watching, watching until the river appeared to stand still, and the bridge felt as if we were sailing upstream. That's when the big kids told me, "If you don't like your report card, throw it over the bridge into the river and tell your mother you lost it."

Following the river up from the bridge in my mind's eye, I often wished I could be swimming "up above white rock," our deep swimming hole, where many of us learned to swim. And following my mind's eye downstream and thinking of the time my father and I canoed right below the Hardwick dam down the Lamoille all the way past Wolcott.

I remember our green iron bridge didn't have that secret place to sit high above the river under the bridge on a granite slab, like the Wolcott Street bridge had, to fish for suckers. They weren't any good anyway.

Sometimes, I walked quickly across our green iron bridge holding my fingers out toward the grating so that they touched each part of the iron latticework or fluttered *The Gazette* across the same grating as I walked across. I remember standing on the bridge, looking up at the high balcony in back of the brick bank building and wondering what Mr. Spaulding— Hardwick's photographer who had his studio on the third floor, with a balcony over-looking the river—felt like before he jumped over the railing to commit suicide.

I remember walking to and from school every day for dinner at noon with the other kids and Mr. Ladd, banker, walking with us. And Dr. Beaupré from his dentist office; Miss Warren from her third grade classroom; and often picking up Eva and Waldo Bemis and Mac McWilliams from their Main Street businesses, as everybody in Hardwick went home for dinner.

So long, old green iron bridge. I know you so well that you are symbolized in my unconscious and come out in my dreams. Years after leaving my daily walk over you, while in the crisis of trying to conquer cancer through excruciating chemotherapy in New York City, I dreamed of you . . . you were something steady to get a hold of. Something that felt permanent. Something that appeared strong and sure in Hardwick. It was winter and the sidewalks were very icy. I dreamed I was trying to walk up the icy incline just before the bridge, close to the Post Office. In my dream I could see my hand reaching out, trying to grab that familiar green iron lattice siding to pull me to safety, as I kept slipping and slipping back on the ice. I had on my L.L. Bean boots but still couldn't get enough traction to grab the rail of that green iron bridge to pull me along to reach the grating. I slipped back and slipped some more. I could even picture my boots trying to grab the ice, but it was no good; I couldn't get a firm grip . . . helplessly slipping."

What a relief to wake up! And realized what we grab when we need something solid and true to hold on to—our childhood memories of daily life—they are always somewhere with us. Well. So long old green iron bridge that is always there. And you will be there for those Hardwickians who know you as so many of us do. We count on you—as our memories will never let you go.

I Remember

❧

CLAUD CROSS,
HARDWICK'S WORKER

"There ain't gonna be no January thaw."

T HIS is the prophet of doom and gloom speaking, the naysayer of conversation:
"Too much winter this year.
I love it.
Everybody says it's gonna be too much winter, water's gonna freeze, price of oil is goin' up, cars slewin' off the roads, ice all piled up on everybody's roof, look up there at that ice!"
"Oh Claude, you know the January thaw will come along and melt it all away!"

"There ain't gonna be no January thaw!"

I remember Claude Cross ever since I was old enough to wander off West Church Street. And one of the first places that we wandered off to in the middle of winter was on the back of the horse-drawn farmer's milk sleigh that would come up over the Wolcott Street bridge, across West Church Street, up North Main, take the first right to the creamery. Early morning. Cold. The horse looked cold. The farmer looked cold. With those frosted eyebrows and runny nose turned to ice he didn't want any little kids adding weight to his load. We ran along the snow-packed road and hopped on anyway. Two or three five- and six-year-olds. The farmer was probably too cold to turn around to make us get off. When we arrived at the creamery, the milk cans were lifted up on the covered platform, they clinked and clanked down the rollers that carried them from below zero early winter morning through strips of black rubber hangings, like a beaded doorway, into a room filled with hot steam that smelled like hot milk . . . and there was Claude. Catching those cans and tossing them around where they needed to go and watch out! Here comes a kid! I remember those frozen rollers, riding, gliding through the rubber strips, right into Claude's domain. And there he was, all dressed in white with a white legionnaire-type cap and acting like we were no different than a can of milk.

Claude worked for Hood's Creamery, out of Boston. In later years, he told me they used to send the milk out by rail, one or two trains a day, and his check came back up from Boston.

Claud was always a worker. He started working early, his first job at Bill Bede's cedar mill right after the Hurricane of '38. He went to work for Hood's in late May 1940. He worked for the Catholic Church for years, inventing a way to cut the grass on those steep slopes. Claude tied a long rope onto his lawn mower, sending it down the hill, and hauling it back up again with the rope. Much later, he worked for my father out at Woodbury, planting Christmas trees.

Claude didn't drive. He was always walking through town. As a young man, he started walking way over to the Woodbury Lake Saturday night dances. He usually got a ride, but he would walk all the 8 miles if he had to.

On the way to and from school, I remember seeing Claude sweeping Hardwick's streets. Conscientiously and particularly, he was out there cleaning the streets, shoveling the snow, and caring for Hardwick as if it were his home.

He worked for the Town of Hardwick most of his life, but I remember him best in later years for taking care of so many family yards, summer and winter. Especially the yards of the widows. My mother, Sally Slayton, depended on him, as did Esther Albee, my aunt Muriel Nichols, Alberta Shattuck, and many more.

Claude Cross was always Hardwick's best care-taker. Everyone wanted him to work for them, because they knew they would never have to call him, or tell him what needed to be done, not to mention they would get the best value for the dollar if Claude was doing the work. He acted like it was his place, and he would know what to do. In fact, it didn't matter if you told him what you wanted done, he only did what he thought was needed. Just ask my Aunt Muriel. He carried her mail up to her every day, cut the grass, and brought the groceries. They carried on a hate-hate relationship for years. And all I heard from my aunt was that Claude "won't do anything right." And all I heard from Claude was, "I quit, I'm not working for her one more day!" Sometimes her lawn would go unmowed for a month, until he felt the grass couldn't get any higher, and back he would go. For the lawn's sake, not the job or the money!

I remember when I first came back to Hardwick in the spring of 1990 and said, "Oh I've got to get Claude to cut my grass (which to Claude meant taking full responsibility for your place year around).

Many said, "Well, you'll never get him, he's got too many people and he won't take on anyone new." Well I knew they didn't know Claude. If he took care of my mother's place, he would take care of mine.

I wasn't there more than two or three days when Claude came around and said, "Well, I don't have your mother to work for anymore, so I'd better cut your grass." When I asked about the snow on the roof in the winter after I closed my house, he replied, "Just leave the snow rake on the porch."

I got to know Claude a lot better when he started taking care of my place. I knew that I never have met anyone who even came close to his prophet of doom and disaster. Which means it was very hard indeed to get a smile out of him. I did. But only twice.

He especially loved to tell about the terrible weather about to hit us, summer or winter. And he must have studied the weather every morning before he left the house because he would give the gloomy picture by paragraphs. One morning in the summer of 1995, I hurried home to write down what he said to me, because it was hard to believe:

"Claude when can you mow my lawn?"

"It won't matter when I mow it. There's no rain in sight, flowers are gonna dry up, grass is turning brown, the river's down in June and the sun's too hot. I guess we're gonna suffer this summer."

The first smile I ever got out of Claude was at the beginning of the summer of 1991, after he had mowed my grass all summer and raked the snow off my porch roof all winter. I asked him what I owed him. He was pushing his lawn mower in front of the Hardwick Inn, just coming across the old green iron bridge, a half circle of sweat dripped from the throat of his T-shirt across his barreled chest, sweat streaming down under the brim of his cap.

"What do I owe you, Claude?"

He reached across his chest into his close-fitting T-shirt pocket, pulled out a piece of paper, turned it over, looked at it a minute, and said, "$16.45."

"$60.45?"

"$16.45!"

"$16.45—for cutting the grass last June, July, and August—and raking snow from the roof all winter?

What's the 45 cents for?"

Smile.

Typical, too, was this day later in 1995, the bluest of skies, the crispest of air, the clearest of sparkling Lamoille River flowing under the bridge.

I was walking downstreet, and Claude was walking upstreet as we crossed at the green iron bridge:

"Isn't this a beautiful day? Now, Claude, even you have to finally admit that this is one beautiful day!"

"Bout time. It won't last. Rain tomorrow. Cold

Monday and Tuesday and I don't know what Wednesday will bring."

Besides the weather, the Hardwick economy was always on Claud's mind. Once instead of responding to the weather he told me that the big milk companies were taking all the profits, the government taxing all the farmers, the price of grain was up, the price of milk had dropped so much that the farmers were all going to bring their milk into town and dump it into the Lamoille.

Oh, Claude! We have missed you in Hardwick ever since you went away to the Greensboro Nursing Home. You knew how to work, and you loved to work. You knew what needed to be done and what was extra that would keep you from caring for someone else's place. You loved to complain. You loved to be best at telling the darkest side of the weather. You were so happy when you could get some happy soul to see the dark side of life—not just the ordinary "good day" stuff for you. But I got you twice! And the second time I even got a hearty laugh.

Once again, I am walking downstreet. And you are coming upstreet. It was in the summer of 1996:

"Awful dry and it's gonna get drier."

"I watered my geraniums this morning and put some Miracle-Gro on them and they perked right up."

"Great stuff."

"What did you say, Claude?"

"Great stuff that Miracle-Gro."

"Why Claude, that's the nicest thing I've ever heard you say in my life."

He threw back his head, laughed with his face to the bright sun, bare gums glistening in the light, and there I had him, Claude—Hardwick's worker—Hardwick's prophet of gloom and doom right there in the sunlight, admitting to life and laughter!

I Remember

❧

EATING OUT DOWNSTREET

Eating out for the Slayton family was for being out of town. I never remember our family going downstreet to eat out. And I never saw or heard of any other family who took their children to a restaurant either. Eating out in Hardwick was for the traveling businessmen without families nearby. Or for couples without children. Or for couples going out without their children. Or for teenagers after the hometown games.

The first time I ever remember eating out in Hardwick (having a lemon-coke with peanut butter-cheese Nabs at Cox's doesn't count) was after a movie at Drown's restaurant. I went into the restaurant with 15 cents (having spent 10 cents for the movie), and ordered a hot dog for 10 cents, and a Barr's Better Beverage orange soda for my last nickel. I sat at the low counter, as you come in the door, and Mr. Drown waited on me. There was a divider between the counter and dining room with tables and chairs—no booths. I can taste it now—it was a steamed, not grilled, hot dog—there isn't another orange flavor that can match Hardwick's own bottling company's orange ... "Barr's Better Beverages." Or their cream or birch beer soda, for that matter. Arthur and Dot Drown lived up over the restaurant and the bakery was there, too. They served breakfast, dinner, and supper; Bill Thompson baked their pies, and Parker Ladd was a short-order cook during summers of his high school years in the 1940's. Drown's place later became an up-scale Mer-Lu's. Burt Stone reminded me that before the war, the restaurant belonged to George Angell, and in the 1920s, Everett and Ethel Campbell owned and ran the restaurant.

The most elegant place to eat out in Hardwick was the Hardwick Inn. I remember looking in through the large window on the way to the green iron bridge, going home after church, and seeing the white linen tablecloths and napkins, just like the Hotel Barre, the Montpelier Tavern, the St. Johnsbury House, or the Darling Inn in Lyndonville—all places where my family had taken me when we were out of town.

Barre, St. Johnsbury, or Hardwick, I didn't have to eat at the Hardwick Inn to know what was served in Vermont's Northeast Kingdom's best hotels. I'll never forget what and how my father always ordered. First of all, we only ate out at the main hotel in town, never at a "stand-alone" restaurant. The waitress handed my dad a menu, which he always put down without looking at it, and asked, "What's the roast for today?" She would reply chicken, pork, or beef, or once in a while, ham, and he would order:

"I'd like a roast pork sandwich . . ."

"That's not on the menu."

Silence.

"Did you want that hot?"

"No gravy, just a <u>little</u> bit of mustard."

"I'll check with the cook." Back from the kitchen, And then we'd go through the pie routine . . .

"Who made the pies?"

"Today?"

"Canned or fresh?"

"I'll take the custard. With a fresh doughnut."

"Mmmmmm," my mother would say, "Hotel coffee." In today's terms that meant Green Mountain coffee . . . the best.

Back in Hardwick, Eva Bemis and Edith Bingham (who married Floyd James) were the waitresses at the Hardwick Inn in 1924, when Eva and

Waldo were first married. Waldo's mother, Eileen
Benjamin, was the manager of the Inn at that time.
J. Leo Johnson owned it, and the Bemis's lived in the
front bedroom upstairs at the Inn. Eva says she can
see them now, four single businessmen came in for
dinner at noon every day always sitting at the same
table, right by the kitchen door. Ed Appolt, publisher
of *The Hardwick Gazette,* Albert Lloyd, undertaker,
Mike Gill from the Hardwick Trust Company, and
Albert Cox, pharmacist. Esther and Judge Melvin
Morse, founders and owners of the M.G. & E. F.
Morse Insurance Company ate dinner there every
day, too. And in the evenings the salesmen who had
come in on the train in the late afternoon, always
had supper at the Inn. Orie Rowell picked them up
with his horse and sleigh or wagon at the train station. He lived in the first house on the right after you
cross the railroad tracks going toward the hospital,
where Ruth Carr later lived. The salesmen gathered
together in the lobby standing around with their sales
samples in hand, talking to each other and spend-
ing the evening together. The candy salesman from
Newport, Mr. Hamlet, claimed the candy was made
in Newport. Shoe salesmen, hat salesmen, hardware
salesmen, everything a Hardwick or neighboring
village store stocked, came in through the salesmen
who stayed at the Hardwick Inn. Typical of the life

of a salesman, Sawyer Lee first came to Hardwick on the train, making the Inn his headquarters. The Balfour salesman hired a horse, or took the stage to Cabot, Greensboro, and Craftsbury, to every town around that had a high school to sell the seniors their class rings. He returned to the Hardwick Inn in the evening, and often stayed a week before returning to his home base in Boston. The lobby was a lively place, Mrs. Babcock, Everett Babcock's mother, sold bus and stage tickets, and she too, ate her noon-day dinner there.

Mr. and Mrs. Ladd, their sons Parker and Keith, ate at the Hardwick Inn in the early 1940's when the Morgan's invited them for a roast chicken dinner every Sunday after Church. That's when Esther Morgan ran the dining room. In the late 1940s, Phyllis Zecchinelli, Hardwick's war bride, remembers when the tourists came through on their way from Burlington to Maine, that "Hardwick was their target." They headed for Cox's Drugstore for a milkshake and the Hardwick Inn for their maple-cured ham dinner. "A trip to Maine wouldn't be the same without the Hardwick stop."

It was in the late '20s that both of Burt Stone's sisters—Harriet and Mildred—waited on table at the Inn. But Burt remembers that his father's favorite restaurant was Bill Robb's. When Burt's mom was away, his dad walked upstreet from the Woodbury Granite Company at noon and met Burt for dinner at Rochelle's, where Bill Robb's mother was the "best cook in town." Bobby Hooper remembers to this day that when his dad bought out the Rochelle kitchen, he ended up with case after case of Utica Club ginger ale that was around for years.

Bruno soon came along and in that space next to the "Bemis 5 and 10 Cent Store," he created the most popular beer parlor—right in the center of Main Street—beside the basement entrance to Charlie Morse's pool hall, and near the other pool hall across the street on the swinging bridge side of the street. Bruno and Eleanor Gajetta planned a different menu each day, and the place was packed the day that "salt pork and milk gravy" were served. A lively entrepreneur, Bruno was always thinking of something new to bring to his customers. Phyllis Zecchinelli remembers when he started a "take-out" business for some holidays in the early 1950s. On Mother's Day the women lined up to come and take out their family's dinner—a real treat for that special day. Mary Isham, later to be Mercier and the proprietor of Hardwick's Diner, Hardwick's most popular eating place, remembers coming down from Craftsbury as a girl and watching people eat lobsters at Bruno's—a fish she'd never heard of, much less seen!

And in 1949, Mary started her restaurant career as waitress at Mrs. Demers's Eagle Hotel, sometimes called the Dew Drop Inn, right across South Main Street from Hardwick Academy. There was a lot of road construction going on around Hardwick and the construction crew stayed at the Eagle Hotel and took their meals there—mostly chicken and steak. But she didn't stay long, as she moved on to work at the Hardwick Inn in 1950. Being eager for new experiences, Mary decided that cooking was what she wanted to do, so she crossed the street and worked at Hollis William's diner as short-order cook, the tiny space between Mer-Lu's and Hill's IGA grocery store. Mary then went on to the big time, working in Stowe for five years before getting homesick for Hardwick.

In the late 1920s and early 1930s, before we had the Hill's IGA on main street, the Cardorsi lunch counter and fruit and vegetable store was there. It was known for its fresh fruit displays, apples all shined, and vegetables arranged in bushel baskets around the place.

And down from Cardorsi's, around the corner, past the drug stores and Freddy Shattuck's paper store, was the Ideal Café, which became Farland's Photography Studio in the late 1940s. Lawrence Shattuck was owner and cook at the Ideal; they were known for ham with pineapple sauce and other sauces that Hardwickians didn't cook at home. Velma and Earleen Lamorey waited on table. Gerald Camp came over from Morrisville and got his start in cooking at the Ideal Café.

Right after the war, Jerry Janiki came to Hardwick, married Bruno's sister Mary, and built Jerry's Dinner (The Village Restaurant). I was in the 8th grade, and got my first paid job at 25 cents an hour (other than working for myself selling Cloverine Salve, Christmas seals, seeds, and delivering *The Burlington Free Press* and *Boston Globe*, and mowing lawns). I had to be there at 4:00 p.m. and work through the supper hour, eating there as well. The job lasted only until basketball season practice started. Besides, I missed my mother's cooking. Years later, in 1966, Mary Mercier bought "The Village Restaurant" from Avon Atkins, Chevy dealer.

At the same time, in 1948 or 1949, Drowns sold their restaurant to Mercedes and Louisa Osuna, which 20 years later became the hot spot for eating out in Hardwick. It burned down soon after they bought it, and a wonderful, new, knotty pine restaurant was rebuilt, with all that pine paneling sprucing up our Main Street, next to Cox's drug store. Everyone was so proud of it. I remember coming back to Hardwick after I was married and taking my New York City husband and friends, the

Irishes, to dinner at Mer-Lu's. Those New Yorkers just couldn't get over how good it was! And how friendly Mercedes and Harold and Louisa and Ray were. They hadn't come from a small town and didn't realize that Mercedes and Louisa had known everyone in Hardwick since they were born.

We always ordered the same thing. Sometimes even getting Hazel Rochester to come with us—and everyone knew she hated going out to eat, except to Mer-Lus for fried clams. Of course she liked Mer-Lu's—she and Mercedes were Hardwick Academy classmates. We all ordered fried clams, French fries, a huge salad, and the biggest Parker House roll any of us had ever seen. And Martinis.

Those were the Martinis and Manhattan days; Harold often brought them over to our table from the bar to talk about New York City. The place was always filled with Hardwick people and many summer people from Greensboro. The Hardwickians all walked over to each other's booths and stood and talked a while. We never went into Mer-Lu's without getting fried clams, or seeing a few people we hadn't come with . . . while the singles sat at the bar and took it all in. People came from St. J. and Barre and Montpelier to eat at Mer-Lu's. Even the summer people and visitors from New York City were impressed.

I Remember

❧

SARAH COBB PHILBROOK

(Letter to the husband of my childhood friend)

26 February, 2018, Sydney, Australia

OH NO Dear Paul. What sad, sad news, my dear, dear, oldest friend in the world—since we were very little girls. Little girls when Sarah lived on Church St. with the Slaytons on one side of the parsonage and the Cobbs on the other. My first memory of a friend was running over to their house to get Sarah to come out and play. And her mother having her sit on a stool in the kitchen to have her long, curly hair put into "Shirley Temple" ringlets. Mrs. Cobb was very methodical, and she combed and combed and combed as I waited and waited and waited for her to finish.

I remember when Sarah came over to my house in 4th or 5th grade after school. I'd get my over-under gun, 22/410, and we'd go across the RR track up on Bridgman Hill, across the brook and into the woods that we knew so well, and I'd shoot chipmunks, and Sarah never wanted her turn.

Sarah showed me the way into reading fiction when I was in 7th grade and she in 8th. The first fiction I ever read, "that I didn't have to read in school," was *Northwest Passage*, Kenneth Roberts, 1937. Whenever I walk into our Jeudevine Library now, I can still see the place she showed me where the best books to read were located. Our library was the only place I went—was allowed to go out after supper—if Sarah were there.

Sarah was the only friend in Hardwick I ever "slept over" with in her bedroom downstairs, in the days when children seldom ate with other families or slept over. When I ate with Sarah at her house, her grandmother, Mrs. Mitchell, did the cooking and the baking: Boston baked beans, brown bread, and Mr. Cobb sometimes made brownies.

Sarah and I shared a paper route that was memorable. We each had an old bike, we picked up the Boston papers and went our separate ways and met back at Freddy Shattuck's to get our quarter pay each Saturday. I remember so well what we did with that

25 cents. Our first stop was to spend 10 cents at the bowling alley where we bowled one string. Then we went to Cox's drug store and spent another 10 cents on an ice cream sundae when Helen Leach was at the soda fountain. Sarah always had chocolate with butterscotch sauce (and the chopped peanuts were a given for which we didn't pay extra), and I had a chocolate with butterscotch . . . with chopped peanuts, just like Sarah. We saved the last nickel of our weekly pay.

In high school we were in the same English, Latin, and French classes. It never occurred to me what it must be like to have your mother for your teacher. Of course, everyone in Hardwick had Mrs. Cobb for a teacher, it was one of those small-town givens. No discussion. And we were varsity basketball. I was the shortest and Sarah was the tallest. I'd grab that ball and shoot it over to Sarah under the basket, and she'd lay it in! In the locker room, I can remember her telling Hazel Hoxie (the superintendent's daughter) jokes that I didn't "get" simply because of their sophisticated vocabulary. Well, they were also a year older . . .

Once when the Hardwick boys' basketball team got into the state finals tournament, my mother drove us to Barre to my great aunts Rachel and Lucy's home to stay overnight in order to go to the BB game. We walked to the big auditorium. At most we were 13 and 14 years old. Sarah also had "old great-aunts" that she had to go and visit on Sundays and holidays. Her family called them the "Wells River Girls," and my family called our great aunts the "Barre folks."

When Sarah went off to college a year ahead of me, I visited her in "Allen House," and she'd tell me what it was like to be in college. One time on my way back to Denison University in Ohio, I stayed over with Sarah in New York City in her "aunt's" apartment. I don't remember the name of the aunt, she wasn't there. I remember well a very upscale, urban, sophisticated furniture and artwork like neither of us had ever seen or even imagined in our whole life. Maybe it was her uncle Fuller's wife? He wasn't from Vermont.

I admired my friend Sarah most when she went to NYC to work with Pan America. The first woman, second person, I ever heard of from Hardwick who worked in NYC. And later, when I lived and worked in "safe and familiar" Connecticut, and was dating Bill Mitchell in NYC, she was the first friend from Vermont to meet him. We met her in her NYC apartment in the village and I knew she approved of Bill because he was an academic, and after all, he was a Mitchell, like her mother. Sarah was in charge of the guest book at our wedding because "she knew how to talk to Bill's NYC friends" as well as our Hardwick people. She told me later that it was easy to tell who was who because the New York women all had on eye makeup, and we Vermonters wouldn't have even dreamed of eye makeup.

Sarah married her perfect Hardwick Academy life-mate. And how I loved visiting them in So. Hero, Vermont on my annual summer trip to Hardwick, in our later years. No one else was as interested in books, travel, and politics as we were. Once again, Sarah was the only Hardwick friend where I "stayed over," in later years in their Florida and Vermont homes and in my Hardwick home.

How we loved driving around our village in the past ten years and up to Greensboro where Paul used to work in the summer on his grandfather's farm. Most of all we drove through the cemetery, and on every street, naming where everyone lived, and which houses were Cobb houses (built by a Cobb), or where our relatives had lived. No question about where we were from . . . we were Hardwick and Hardwick Academy through and through.

I will remember my very first friend Sarah always. I miss her very much.

I Remember

❧

CHRISTMAS EVE SHOPPING

With my Father, 1944

I MUST have been 11. I remember Mr. Cox himself, who was as quiet as the new pharmacist. I remember him mostly for selling my father a Christmas present for my mother every Christmas Eve.

We walked in, straight over to the jewelry counter by the grandfather clock that stood in the window for everyone to see the time as they walked upstreet. Without a spoken word between them, Mr. Cox leaned down to open his safe, took two jewelry boxes out, put them up on the glass counter to show my father. He opened each box, my dad pointed to one, Mr. Cox nodded, put the other one back in the safe, nodded my father's selection to

Helen who worked the soda fountain opposite the jewelry counter, she gift-wrapped it (the only place I ever saw a gift wrapped at the store instead of at home), my dad paid cash to Mr. Cox—still no words spoken—took the store-wrapped gift home, walked right into our living room and placed it on the upper branches of our balsam Christmas tree.

One year he chose a necklace of two colors of gold. Another year, a floral pin of two colors of gold, and then I remember the bracelet of two gold colors. There was another floral pin of two colors of gold plus pearls. I never remember anything except two colors of gold. I remember my mother opening those two-colored gold pieces expressing such delight and surprise to my father. And yet. Each day after Christmas she said to me, "You know I can never wear gold; it turns my skin green . . . I'll just have to paint this piece with colorless nail polish."

I Remember

⁓

JEUDEVINE LIBRARY

I MUST have been nine years old. Ten, maybe. Going into fifth grade. Perly Shattuck was town clerk. I had been walking up West Church Street by the library all summer and watching with envy the big boys mowing that great library lawn. I knew they got 50 cents for the job. I knew that 50 cents added to my weekly allowance of 10 cents would give me a real boost, money-wise. I crossed the street to the Memorial Building, walked into the town clerk's office, and asked, "Do you have to be a boy to mow the library lawn?"

"Why, no, you can cut it next week," said Perly Shattuck as he swirled around in his swivel captain's chair Always formal, and easily one of the best-dressed men in Hardwick, never without a white shirt, bow tie, dark suit, he and barber Bert Cobb were the only ones I knew who walked briskly downstreet, swinging their umbrellas as if they were walking sticks.

The next Saturday I got my dad's lawn mower out of the barn; the handle hit me at eye level rather than at waist level for which it was designed. Pushing that lawn mower with hands raised about my shoulders was the task for the day, although I was not yet aware of that challenge. I eagerly pushed the mower up West Church in the cool of the morning of a very hot day. I got started right in front of the library, which has just a little slope to the sidewalk, adding some variety to the job (compared to the Catholic Church lawn, which had a really steep lawn where a rope had to be tied to the lawn mower and Claude Cross stood at the top of the hill and just "let her roll" strip by strip, to cut the lawn). After an hour of the easy stuff, I decided to wait and do the sloping parts later and moved to the back between the library and Father Miller's home (the Episcopal minister). Back and forth, back and forth, this lawn mower is getting heavier and heavier . . . the clock face of the Methodist Church moved slower and slower . . . it took forever to strike.

I felt like a very little girl by the third hour, and

the handle seemed too high to even reach. Three hours went by. It's so hot. I'm so thirsty. I'm not really done. Four hours. Now I'm really thirsty. I wonder if I could run home to get a drink of water? That sloping part isn't done yet. I think I'll go home and get a drink of water! Maybe I'll take the lawn mower with me. I'll come back later. I'm not really finished.

I remember Jeudevine. It's the place where I never finished the job I started. I remember Jeudevine. I never collected my 50 cents. I remember Jeudevine. That's the place where I learned that some jobs look easier than they are.

Luckily for me, the outside of the library had nothing to do with the inside. I don't think Mrs. Hooper, our librarian, ever knew about the lawn-mowing story. Or at least she didn't act like she knew it. I remember going to the library and having my own library card by first grade. I often sat in the reading room looking at the magazines. It was the first time I ever saw special magazines for kids. I especially remember *Jack and Jill*, which had great puzzles in it. And stories that we second and third graders could read all by ourselves.

And it wasn't long after that, probably in sixth grade, that Sarah Cobb showed me the grown-up books in the library. She was the best reader I knew, and my friend who knew most about books. She showed me where all the good stories and authors were. She was a year ahead of me in school and seemed like a lifetime ahead of me in knowing the best books to read. I can see them on the shelves right now—take a left at Mrs. Hooper's desk, and on the first right as you enter the stacks, look about one-third up and there was a whole shelf length of Kenneth Roberts's historical novels. Sarah's favorites. *Northwest Passage* was the first grown-up book I remember reading. Robert's *Trending into Maine, March to Quebec, Henry Gross* and his *Dowsing Rod*, and *The Battle of Cowpens* all followed as I learned to "go through" one writer whom I liked.

I can't remember if Mrs. Hooper kept the reproduction books behind the desk or if we found them in the card catalog without asking, but in junior high school we girls had books in hand, looking in awe at the illustrations. Of course we never dreamed of asking to take them out, or of putting our name on the loan card.

When I got to the seventh grade, the library was the only place my dad would let me go on a school night (Tuesdays). Alan Hovey, the new coach's son, would meet me there and we would stand out of Mrs. Hooper's sight, whispering to each other and thinking how smart we were to be alone in the library stacks . . . Oh Jeudevine. Oh, wisdom of books. Oh, adventures of youth.

I Remember

◦

EVA BEMIS

"Where've you been??" was her usual greeting when I'd come into her home office for a quick visit during my summer days in Hardwick. I remember Eva Bemis best after 1989, when I bought my Hardwick home and moved back for the summers. As widows, she and my mother could see each other's house lights and keep track of each other's comings and goings. It was Eva whom my mother called in the middle of the night when she had a heart attack. It was Eva who followed the Rescue Squad in her car to the Morrisville hospital, 14 miles away.

Eva and I go way back. We were "across the street" neighbors. She claims I used to wake her up in the morning when as a 3- or 4-year old I'd go noisily up and down the sidewalk in my mother's high heels. She lived with husband Waldo, her mother, Mrs. Bardelli, and their wire-haired Terrier, Caesar (of whom there were several). Eva and Waldo walked to the store every day and we kids on the street often walked downstreet with them on our way to school. As we walked along West Church Street, we'd pick up Mr. Ladd, banker, and Dr. Beaupré, Hardwick's dentist.

Eva's birthday was on January 17, the same birthday as my dad. My mother always invited Eva and Waldo for a birthday dinner together, so I grew up with a family birthday tie as well as knowing her in the store and as a neighbor.

There Eva would sit at her desk where she could look up West Church Street, watching cars drive and people walk by going to and from Wolcott Street, talking to Phyllis or Margaret and Lady, or Marvene, or Lorraine Hall or Danny with his grandchildren. She loved watching golf, if she were alone. When Marjorie Barr was visiting, or someone from out-of-town, they'd have tea in the living room. Looking out at the beautiful view of Buffalo Mountain. The rest of us stayed in the office, wall safe behind her with the Hardwick United Church's Sunday collection stored safely until Monday along with her "books." There were photos on the wall of the 1940s, of Waldo and Eva and Caesar walking down our street. "Parker Ladd took that picture when he was a schoolboy at Hardwick Academy."

I love the way she walked. I'd say to friends, "It's interesting to see how most older people move—Eva walks so quickly and surely, never looks down, hasn't changed a bit in her walk. She goes up and down stairs as if she were 50 instead of 80 something." I love the way she cooked and enjoyed her meals. If I dropped by during her lunch or dinner, she'd be enjoying a special meal and reading a book or magazine at the table. When she was alone, which was most of the time, she was always doing something interesting. She never bought a dryer; Eva hung her clothes down cellar in the winter and outdoors on the line in summer. She appreciated her daily life more than most of us do—not wasting them wishing for days gone by, nor worrying about the future. She exercised in winter by walking laps around her cellar.

On Sundays after church, and the money was collected (she was treasurer for as long as she lived) she'd always say, "Let's go up to the cemetery and drive around." Our Hardwick Cemetery has many specially carved stones because Hardwick was a granite center. The Scotts immigrated to Hardwick in the 1800s from Aberdeen, for the quarrying of granite. The Italians came to carve the stone. And so, here I was, back in Hardwick, and Eva reminded me that's what we do on Sunday afternoons.

My Ford red ranger was in her yard. Eva jumped right in and both of us got out to walk around and look at the Bemis and Slayton gravestones, talk about growing up in Hardwick, Hardwick Academy, the Hardwick Inn, basketball, and during the war when Waldo organized the Junior Commandos on our street. He taught us how to march, to "about face," to stay in line and stay in step. I was the only girl in the 6- to 10-year-olds Junior Commandos of West Church Street.

Back in the pick-up on our way out she looked around that cemetery and each stone would bring back memories and stories. Then she would say, "No, go that way! Look at my sister Angie's stone, my father carved that little girl in stone. She died at three years old. I was named Angie after her, Angie Eva." And then we'd go on, leaving the cemetery to go back home. I'd rush off home, and she'd always say, "Going so soon?" no matter how long or short a time I was there, those were always Eva's parting words.

I Remember

❧

EULOGY FOR
SALLY SLAYTON

My Mother
February 22, 1906—November 24, 1986

My first memory of my mother was from the bathtub. I must have been about three years old. She stood back, hands on hips, tilted head, projected voice, and said, "Harry! Put down that varnish can! Did you swallow it? Oh me oh my, it's hard enough to get the dirt off the outside, how on earth will we ever get it off the inside? Well. You'll have to swallow some sandpaper—there, there, don't cry . . . see? The gentleman is giving you a penny . . ."

My mother was practicing her monologue to be given that evening at a church or Women's Club or

Fortnightly Club event. I loved to hear her practice at home. Her stories well-learned from her teenage elocution course at Stanstead College, Canada, right over the Canadian border a short distance from Newport, Vermont, her hometown. My mother gave another performance of that same monologue standing in one of the world's most beautiful formal gardens: the Paris Garden of Luxembourg, just for me on my 50th birthday.

I remember my mother driving Church Street kids to Eligo every day in the summer. She was the only mother I ever saw swimming. She did a perfect sidestroke. Until I left Hardwick for college, I never saw any grown-up or kid ever do a sidestroke.

I remember my mother taking her walk each day down to my father's garage, arms swinging, speed-walking as if in training for the Olympics—in the '30s and '40s—long before walking and jogging were trendy. She made a big circle in the garage yard and fast-tracked right back home. "One mile each way," she always said.

I remember my mother as a homemaker. Washing our clothes every Monday, ironing every Tuesday—baked a fresh pie and four donuts every day because my father wouldn't eat them a day old. My mother loved being married to George Slayton. She loved being his homemaker. They loved their search for the perfect food in season: dandelion greens along the streams where my father fished for trout, new peas, maple syrup, and they drove way over to Middlebury (80 miles each way) for the first blackberries of the season.

I remember my mother as the most gracious hostess in Hardwick. As two o'clock every afternoon she changed her clothes, got out her tea cups from her most beautiful teacup collection, and Mrs. Hall or Mrs. Ladd came across the street for afternoon tea before their children got home from school.

I remember my mother setting a beautiful table, creative centerpieces and wildflowers in our home— black-eyed Susans were her favorite. I remember the dinner parties when Jay and I would lie on the floor above the living room, ear to the register, and listen to the jokes and stories and heated discussions on religion and politics below. My last three visits to Hardwick included my mother's special luncheons given in her usual elegance; age made no difference in her style.

I remember my mother most of all as proper. With impeccable manners. And she expected her daughter to be just as proper. She cringed when she heard my voice rise above all others at Hardwick Academy's basketball games. She always sat up straight. I picture her on the edge of a chair, perfect posture while drinking the hottest tea anyone could put to their lips. My mother always wore hat and gloves, even after hats were out of style, she set her own style, telling me that "you can wear the same suit for years, as long as it's a good one." My mother was a woman with a lot of class.

I remember my mother standing at the stove, wooden spoon to her mouth, tasting her vegetable soup or beef stew—a twinkle in her eye, smacking her lips and saying, "Oh that's so good!" She loved creative cooking. I think of her apple pie. I know exactly how it looks, tastes, and how much liquid is in each forkful of that pie. I remember my mom's mincemeat pie, filled cookies, cucumber pickles, lobster bisque, corn chowder, johnny cake, and apple sauce. Her rhubarb pie, berry pies, fig squares, and cottage pudding.

I remember my mother as a woman who loved the city. She wanted me to love it, too. My mother took me by train to Boston to visit her cousin, to see my first play, and go to my first concert at 10 years old. She and my father took us, too, to Boston's Chinatown, Boston's Union oyster house, Montreal's French pastries, and to NYC's delis for hot pastrami on rye with dill pickles—long before Hardwick knew ethnic foods—after the war and before television.

I remember my mother as a woman who loved life. She's an extraordinary enthusiastic model: actively making the best of "what is." She loved fun—and found thousands of occasions for laughter. She loved her home and she loved being on the road. She couldn't wait to get to the next lunch, friend, dinner, church service, or person she met on the way.

My mother had no regrets. She told me on her death bed that she was hoping that she and my father's car would come out even, but that the car had given out first. My brother John calls her "Little Sally Sunshine." She was always out front radiating cheer, optimism, and wishing well to every single person she encountered. Children, too.

I remember my mother as a woman who loved to take a trip. My father would come home and say, "Sally! Get ready!! We're going to Boston, to Burlington, to Montreal or to call on a farmer about a tractor…"

And like all those trips with my dad, she was always ready to go—and to her later trips to Florida with my brother Jay, and to Europe with my brother John. I am confident that my mother was very well prepared and ready to go—from West Church Street in Hardwick … to Eternity.

ALSO BY JOYCE SLAYTON MITCHELL

Who is This Kid? Colleges Want to Know!
Critical Thinking Co., 2019

The Chinese Guide to American Universities, Wenhui Zhu
Zhenrong, Shanghai (Mandarin Language), 2016

The Korean Guide to American Universities,
(Korean Language), 2014

The Indian Guide to American Colleges,
HayHouse, Mumbai, India, 2010

Eight First Choices: Strategies for Getting Into College,
SuperCollege, 2009, Third Edition, 2017, in press 2021

*Paris by Pastry: Stalking the Sweet Life on the Streets
of Paris,* Jones Books, 2006

Bible Express: Fast Track to the Old and New Testaments,
St. Paul Press, 2006

Winning the Heart of the College Admissions Dean,
Ten Speed Press, 2002, 2005

Knuckle boom-Loaders Load Logs, Overlook Press, 2003

Tractor-Trailer Trucker
Tricycle Press, 2002, 2nd printing spring 2000

Crashed, Smashed, and Mashed: Junkyard Heaven
Tricycle Press, spring 2001

A Special Delivery: Mother/Daughter Letters from Afar,
Equilibrium Press, 1999

The College Board Guide to Career Planning,
The College Board, 1990, 1994

Winning the Chemo Battle, Norton, 1986, trade edition, 1988

The Guide to Canadian Universities, Simon & Schuster, 1970

The Guide to College Life, Prentice-Hall, 1969

About the Author

∾

BORN AND RAISED IN HARDWICK, Joyce Slayton Mitchell's focused career was built on more than 35 years as Director of College Advising in America's public and independent schools of Connecticut, New Jersey, and New York City. Expert in U.S. college admissions, writer, lecturer, and consultant to schools and education systems, Mitchell left the Nightingale-Bamford School in NYC for more adventure in China. She worked in Shenzhen, Beijing, and Shanghai bringing AP curriculum into the public schools until 2015. She then consulted with Chinese college admissions entrepreneurs until 2019, when she left China at the beginning of the pandemic. She currently works remotely with U.S. and Chinese students applying to American colleges.